*Poetry and Politics
in the Works
of Rainer Maria Rilke*

Translated from the German
*Das verschluckte Schluchzen: Poesie und
Politik bei Rainer Maria Rilke*
Copyright 1972 by Athenäum-Verlag GmbH, Frankfurt, with
the authorization of Akademische Verlagsgesellschaft,
Athenaion, Wiesbaden, Federal Republic of Germany

Copyright © 1981 by Frederick Ungar Publishing Co., Inc.
Printed in the United States of America

Designed by H. Roberts Design

Library of Congress Cataloging in Publication Data
Schwarz, Egon, 1922–
  Poetry and politics in the work of Rainer Maria Rilke.
  Translation of: Das verschluckte Schluchzen.
c1972.
  Bibliography: p.
  Includes index.
  1. Rilke, Rainer Maria, 1875–1926—Political
and social views.   I. Title.
PT2635.I65Z862613   831'.912   81-2692
ISBN 0-8044-2811-5   AACR2

Poetry and Politics in the Works of Rainer Maria Rilke

Egon Schwarz

TRANSLATED BY DAVID E. WELLBERY

FREDERICK UNGAR PUBLISHING CO.
NEW YORK

For Claire and Herbie Lindenberger

Contents

	Preface to the English Edition	*vi*
Chapter 1	**The Problem**	*1*
Chapter 2	**Early Impressions**	*5*
Chapter 3	**World War**	*24*
Chapter 4	**Period of Maturity**	*42*
Chapter 5	**Lyric Poetry and Politics**	*88*
Chapter 6	**Conclusion**	*114*
	Notes	*120*
	Index	*158 & 159*

Preface to the English Edition

I was tempted to play at Bernard Shaw and write a "Foreword for Americans" to this book, but after some reflection decided against the idea. It is best that the text stand on its own. May I say in general terms only that this is a book about presuppositions: the thoughts and beliefs, partly factual and based on scientific knowledge, mostly mythical and ideological, that are shared by an age. Of course, such assumptions are not universal. Depending on geography, on religious, ethnic and linguistic traditions, political structures, social class, and the historical moment, individuals have a wide array of ideas to choose from.

Rainer Maria Rilke, one of the celebrated poets of this century, is at the center of this inquiry. Its aim is to show that even great poetry, esoteric and seemingly timeless as Rilke's, is part of the emotional and intellectual system of defenses that serves the individual's need to orient himself in a world of impenetrable complexities.

The investigation that follows is not directed against Rilke, not even against such weaknesses as his much observed "snobbism" and his attraction to the aristocracy; nor has it been written to diminish Rilke scholarship, which is variegated and in part excellent. At the most, my study deplores an occasional abdication of critical thinking and the adoption of idolatry or hagiography as approaches by some scholars. It does seek to show that poetry is not a solitary force springing from the inwardness of an autonomous mind, but that it is written in a language belonging to recognizable historical circumstances. It proceeds from the assumption that human beings are of necessity affected by the climate of history. To make this point, the intellectual development of a poet par excellence—who also lived what many contemporaries regarded as the typical "lifestyle" of a poet and whom they regarded as the living embodiment of poetry in their time—is recapitulated in its dependence on socio-historical givens. The study shows the connections between a consciousness that considered itself hermetic and autarchic and the social-psychological constellations of the world surrounding it.

The point of departure is the little-known *Lettres Milanaises* written by Rilke toward the end of his life to an Italian duchess, in which he emphatically welcomes Benito Mussolini to the European scene. To understand this enthusiasm, the book retraces the stages of Rilke's growth from his childhood in Prague and the military academies, the love affair with Lou Andreas-Salomé, and the trips to Russia, the Paris of Rodin and Cézanne, World War I, and its revolutionary aftermath, to Muzot, Rilke's castlelike retreat in Switzerland. Step by step his views are reconstructed, their foundation and function examined, their limitations exposed and, last but not least, their presence in his famous *oeuvre*, from the Prague stories to the *Duino Elegies* and the *Sonnets to Orpheus*, rediscovered.

The text of the present English version deviates from the original German only in details. Author and translator collaborated to produce a simpler, clearer, and more readable text, attuned to the needs of the Anglo-American reader, who is seldom familiar with the historical substratum into which Rilke has been placed here. All quotations

PREFACE TO THE ENGLISH EDITION

from the work of Rilke, and from that of critics and contemporaries, have been translated for this volume, unless otherwise specified in the notes. Such a careful rendering is the exception rather than the rule. It would not have been possible without a translation subsidy from Washington University, with which the author has been affiliated for many years. Thanks are also due to the many friends, benevolent readers, and favorable reviewers whose reception of the German original has made an English version desirable.

E.S.

Chapter 1
The Problem

Over the years the hagiographic and critical literature on Rainer Maria Rilke has grown to fill entire libraries. Most of it reads as if the poet had lived on a planet remote from our own earth so afflicted by famine, inflations, wars, and revolutions. In many exegeses Rilke appears as if surrounded by the halo of a religious leader whose sayings are submitted to the subtlest methods of theological interpretation. Whole books have been written about the complex meanings of single words that Rilke employed in a manner deviating from normal linguistic usage.[1] There have also been, of course, heated disputes over the reconstruction of his doctrine such as are familiar in the history of every sect. Today, thanks to these efforts, the enormous metaphorical edifice of the Prague prophet is for the most part clearly delineated. In today's world it is something of a spectacular Taj Mahal of poetry that stands functionless in its environment, gaped at uncomprehendingly by the curious.

Rilke himself is in the main responsible for the fact that scholars have isolated his work from the actual destinies of his contemporaries and from the intellectual attempts to comprehend them. It is not just that he concerned himself hardly at all with contemporary events or expressed himself with little clarity on the issues about which men were literally tearing one another apart; such aloofness he shares with many creative minds of his day. Beyond this practical disinterest, though, he actually made a principle of his estrangement from the events that so shook the age. Such protective distancing is exhibited—to choose one example—in a letter to a young admirer living in Milan, the Duchess Gallarati Scotti, who appealed for his advice about the political exigencies besetting her family and her homeland. "As far as the world of politics is concerned," Rilke avers, "I stand so distant from it and feel so incapable of grasping its movements and countermovements that it would be ridiculous for me to express myself about any event lying in its domain, whatever it might be."[2]

In this admission there is, of course, a good deal of truth and it is not at all the aim of this inquiry to contradict it. Rather, I intend here to follow a course that runs counter to the predominant direction of Rilke scholarship in order to bring into view the entanglements that bind the poet and his *oeuvre* to the social conditions of his time. It will turn out that these connections are not at all as hidden as one might have supposed and that it is mainly the standpoint of the viewer that determines which portion of the scenery emerges into the foreground. I proceed from the premise that the problem of what position to adopt vis-à-vis the social tensions and conflicts of one's age is not eliminated by the mere assertion of one's impartiality.[3] Indeed, in the twentieth century the very decision to remain apolitical constitutes a political fact of the first order from which alone a whole set of political attitudes can be inferred. Since we will of necessity use the term "political" on several occasions in what follows, it is advisable to limit the term to a precise meaning. We shall adopt the definition offered by Helmut Kreuzer: "By politics we do not only mean in this context an action which is theoretically and practically oriented toward power values. We shall allow the concept

THE PROBLEM

to embrace rather the entirety of evaluative utterances having to do with political and social orders, institutions and movements (be they real, ideal, fictional, or propagated) and the entirety of actions which are immediately directed toward apologetics or criticism vis-à-vis such orders, or toward their maintenance, modification or destruction, or toward the realization of new orders."[4]

Thus one is hardly surprised when Rilke—disregarding the apolitical credo he has just espoused—proclaims to the same correspondent his approval of the Italian fascist regime with its deprivation of freedom and its acts of violence, praising Mussolini as the "architect of the Italian will," as the "smith forging a consciousness that blazes up anew at the flames of an ancient fire." "Happy Italy,"[5] he acclaims the nation that had witnessed the terrorist acts of the fascist commandos and—to the horror of everyone the times had not yet fully brutalized—the assassination of the peace-loving member of parliament, Giacomo Matteotti.[6]

Yet, it is adamantly not a question here of registering retrospective moral indignation, but rather of attempting to discover exactly how Rilke arrived at such conceptions, what symptomatic value they possess within the totality of his world view, and how they relate to other ideas expressed in his correspondence or shaped in his poetic works. One can legitimately charge previous Rilke scholarship with having neglected this task. With few exceptions, critics have calmly ignored the support of Mussolini avowed in the *Lettres Milanaises* and have implied thereby that such a defamation of political freedom has nothing at all to do with the definition of human existence the poet so passionately endeavored to achieve in the *Duino Elegies* and the *Sonnets to Orpheus*; or that Rilke's peculiar attitude toward poverty is entirely unrelated to the political measures which in fascist Italy met with his obvious approval.

For this is the second premise of my inquiry: in the intellectual encounter with, and appropriation of life—especially in the case of such a sincerely striving and creative human being as Rilke—all things are interconnected and an interpretation of social life, once adopted, will produce resonances even in the most sublime lyric regions. In this regard it approaches distortion to speculate again and again *ad nauseam* about one thought and at the same time modestly to conceal another. In such one-sidedness, attitudes and standpoints of a likewise political nature—in the broadest sense of the term—are revealed. Real significance is grasped when disparate elements are related to one another in a convincing way.

My choice of theme, however, is equally intended to oppose another sort of arrogance often encountered today. It simply won't do to dispose of a figure from the immediate past whom we vaguely sense to be embarrassing, outdated. This is mere presumptuousness. Regarding a phenomenon like Rilke, neither anxious concealment nor complaisant sarcasm will suffice; what is called for is a broadly conceived effort at understanding. His very example provides us with an insight that remains salutary today: that even those who deem themselves above everything mundane are bound up in the texture of their historical situation. Finally, I also hope that the tracing of these interconnections will contribute to an understanding of Rilke's *oeuvre* in all its facets.

Chapter 2
Early Impressions

What social milieu a writer comes from is not necessarily of crucial importance. Even Marxist critics—as long as they have maintained the slightest intellectual flexibility—do not insist on a correspondence between social origins and class consciousness. Of course, one's origins are influential in determining how one views the world's panorama, but the decisive factor is the quality of one's early impressions and the manner in which the elements of empirical experience are ordered by the artistic imagination. Where an individual gets his talent and why he believes this or that can seldom be established unequivocally.

How, then, did social reality present itself to the child René (which was Rilke's given name until Lou Andreas-Salomé changed it to Rainer)? In seeking to answer this question we have to rely on two sources: the available research findings regarding the poet's origins and Rilke's own retrospective view especially as revealed in the youthful works of the newly emancipated writer still occupied by the problems of his home. Rilke's Prague environment and the social circumstances of his family have often been described.[1] We need only briefly review the essential points.

Rilke's parents, however different and even incompatible they might have been, shared at least one characteristic: they both were among the socially dissatisfied, the "losers" of modernity. To be sure, the mother was from the city's patrician class. Her parents lived in solid, almost elegant surroundings, several details of which impressed themselves on the admiring grandson. But Phia, his mother, had married a man who was her social inferior and who, in addition, proved himself over the years to be something of a failure. As a young man he had projected a degree of elegance and flair. A member of the German bourgeoisie, he automatically belonged to Prague's most prominent class and could allow himself certain expectations. His family had several influential state officials and other successful careers to its credit. In fact, René's uncle Jaroslav was later elevated to the nobility, thereby inching a notch closer to that aristocratic world of success Rilke's parents so longed for. But René's father turned out to be a thoroughly inappropriate vehicle for the soaring social aspirations of his spouse. Actually he had wanted to become an officer but had to abandon this career and instead accept the subaltern station of a civil servant, a position he would remain in for the rest of his life. That his yearnings remained oriented toward the more glamorous regions of the officer class can be inferred from the fact that he sent his ten-year-old son to a military academy.

The domestic atmosphere, then, was permeated by the tortuously unfulfilled ambitions of the parents, and there can be no doubt that this atmosphere deeply impressed the highly sensitive child. After all, the social sciences have taught us how the social-historical situation of parents—which even in them produces distinct psychological correlates—is transformed in the child into psychic structures. As the child grows out into the world, these structures develop into social attitudes and in this way social position and psychological reactions are complexly intertwined.

How then did the young Rilke react to the social-psychological configurations of his background? First of all, by rebelling against the Germanophile attitudes of his parents. They shared with their class, along with several other prejudices, a disdain for the oppressed Slavic population.[2] By throwing away this nationalistic crutch, René Rilke liberated himself from many aspects of the social myth that held sway over his immediate surroundings. His own search for freedom as well as his quest for poetic inspiration took on the form of a pronounced sympathy for the Slavic masses around him. There is an aesthetic justification for this: "That is the tragic fate of all German poets in my native city. If they wish to draw their inspiration from the people, they disappear under the flood of a strange nationhood, and draw their stimulus and atmosphere from the intrinsic being of the Czechs, whose fruitful influence surrounds them from all sides."[3]

In Rilke's early works this rebellion is embodied in various ways, most notably in his treatment of the German element of Prague. Wherever he attempted imaginatively to evoke his home city—for instance, in the collection of novellas *Along the Edge of Life*[4] or in the posthumous tale *Ewald Tragy*[5]—the Germans inevitably appear as soulless figures inhabiting a deathlike atmosphere, totally rigidified in their memories, habits, and thought patterns, always inclined away from life and toward death. Ridiculous in all that, they seem most ridiculous on account of the nationalistic arrogance that so markedly contrasts with their otherwise unalloyed vacuousness. This mode of depicting the Germans is most effective in the second of the *Two Stories of Prague*, the novella "The Siblings." There, glaring contrasts make the poet's intentions clear. The world of the German aristocracy and bourgeoisie is rendered satirically, the Czech world romantically. The figures of the somewhat imbecilic Colonel Meering von Meerhelm and his status-conscious spouse Charlotte, with their ossified social and national self-conceit, stand out from their Slavic surroundings like grotesque caricatures. The sole German in the novella on whom a conciliatory light falls is the young pharmacist Ernst Land, who—not unlike Rilke—distances himself from his German social background.[6] He preserves the childhood memory of only one woman, no doubt his mother, who "sang tender Slavic songs,"[7] and in the end marries the Slavic heroine of the tale. The reader is offered the hope of a symbiosis in which the German element, despite all the previous ridicule, finally comes to play a dignified role.

But we must look at the Czech inhabitants of this world as well. They too are variously rendered and share in the ambivalence that suffuses the text. We can distinguish here between three basic types. First of all, there are the dignitaries of the National Café. Satisfied with their social position, these figures are Czechs in name only and for that reason are treated contemptuously by the author. When the Czech liberation movement begins to take action, these dignitaries are nearly as quick and adamant in their rejection of it as are the German upper classes.[8]

Juxtaposed to them are the heroic Czech nationalists whose romantic rebelliousness shines with a certain splendor. Still, there is something immature and—despite their radicalism—aimless about them. There can be no doubt that they too, apart from certain vague sympathies, are rejected by the author. Their leader is the agitator Rezek, a Machiavelli or Savonarola figure, who in his fanaticism either misapprehends or feels contempt for all manifestations of genuine life. Rezek is only half convinced of his own political goals: "The dream of this dark man was to find young people from a good class who, persuaded of the justice of their enterprise, would strive for national liberation with the blind bearlike force of their conviction and who with youthful relentlessness would pursue a goal that he himself could not always believe in."[9] Through statements like this, the movement Rezek leads is discredited in the eyes of the reader.

The life story of the young Zdenko Wanka affords insight into the dilemma of the Czech nationalist revolutionaries. Brooding, estranged from the lighter joys of life, he feels attracted to the revolutionaries and their ideals even though he can detect nothing of an alleged "enslavement" of the Czech people: "He wondered how it could have happened that over the years he had noticed none of this oppression. . . . Now he actually believed on occasion that he perceived an oppressed, enslaved figure, but, as soon as he took a closer look, he recognized dejectedly that it was merely the burden of poverty or misery and not the yoke of servitude that bent the stranger's shoulders."[10] When Wanka discovers that the rebels' driving spirit, the student Rezek, acts not out of conviction but out of a desire for sheer power, he inwardly withdraws from them. And yet he has already invested too much of his life in the movement to be able to recover from this disillusionment. Given the entire arrangement of the narrative, there remains little else for him to do but to disappear from the scene as quickly as possible. The author disposes of him in a few sentences by having him locked up in a prison where he contracts pneumonia and dies.

For whose sake has this promising Czech youth been swept from the stage? For the sake of the third group: the anonymous People, embodied here in the figure of Zdenko's sister Luisa. This character first appears as rather sickly but, following her brother's death, progressively blossoms into health and happiness. Like the eponymous hero of the novella "King Bohusch," she represents the Slavs in their sensibility, tenderness, and soulfulness, in their connectedness with the past and in their almost poetic imaginative capacity. Initially she passes through the same stages as her erring brother. Surrounded by the harmonious landscape of provincial Bohemia, she lives an entirely unproblematic life with her family. In this idyll of the *ancien régime* her father holds the position of a royal forester, and the national conflicts and other characteristic diseases of modern life have yet to show themselves. With the death of the father, the family is forced to move to the city where they settle in a proletarian tenement house, the traditional milieu of the dispossessed. It is here that the real problematic of the narrative emerges. The very first page of the story emphasizes the "manorial"[11] impression the Wanka family's furniture makes on the simple people of the neighborhood. Especially noteworthy are Rilke's remarks on the maid's belief in ghosts and her reaction to the absence of such superstitions among the inhabitants of Prague: "Rosalka habitually felt contempt for whoever didn't believe in such things. She considered it a lack of cultivation and experience, one of the many evil consequences of the ever more powerful 'big city' culture." Of course this is intended as humorous, but the slightest familiarity with the poet would reveal that the apostrophes were really unnecessary: Rilke thoroughly shared the maid's aversion for metropolitan culture. Since the ghostly apparitions in question here first occurred in the "Krummauer Castle," one can already discern in this early novella a set of polarities that will prove characteristic for Rilke's later work—*Malte*, for example— as well as for his life: sophisticated Paris and country castles, spiritualism and materialism, tradition and rejected modernism, childhood of security and exposure in a Babel of sin—a series that could be continued endlessly. There is, to be sure, nothing new in all this; such opposites had been around for a considerable time and had long since acquired a political significance. What is interesting for our inquiry is to observe how early Rilke adopted a socially conservative attitude that identifies itself as "apolitical."

Like her brother, Luisa joins the Czech movement and even passes through an infatuation with the power-hungry Rezek who, in his obstinancy, notices nothing of this miracle. The death of the brother leaves both mother and daughter in a state of psychological paralysis and confusion out of which each eventually finds her own path back to

EARLY IMPRESSIONS

life. The mother recalls her protective, parental function and attempts to provide Luisa with training as a teacher of French and piano. True to an old Czech practice, she acquires the financial means for this undertaking by going to work in the homes of the German upper class. After the loss of the higher ambitions she had reserved for her son, she is content to prepare her daughter for a less glamorous existence. With this characterization, the author seems to intend a critique of the older generation of Czechs who accommodated themselves to their fate. But in the case of Luisa he has a much more sublime solution in mind. Through her long illness she gradually regains her resources until, during a symbolic springtime walk, the once-so-frail and now-so-healthy maiden is identified with the reawakening force of nature, which in turn coalesces with the upward-striving Slavic people. We know the outcome well: once the different types that fail to conform to the author's ideals have been removed from the narrative through plausible deaths of various kinds, a shining Slavic People, attractive in every respect, triumphantly lays claim to a future which, without revolution, is quite naturally its own. "I'd like to learn to speak German better," Luisa suggests, "perhaps you could use some Bohemian in exchange."[12] Through this incipient Berlitz School those Germans blessed with internal spirituality are allowed to share in the joys of the future.

Rilke's sympathy for the Czech liberation movement and his simultaneous reservations vis-à-vis nationalist activism are expressed much more forthrightly in an early poem:

Sounds of Freedom

Bohemian People! Among your circles
a new genius awakens
ancient, hot songs of freedom,
and they call out in no faint

> words that your iron chains
> must be entirely smashed.
>
> These poets of strife blow
> enticingly; and you can strike
> to pieces, people, in your rage
> the marble vases of the law,
> and yet from their empty phrases
> you can't build yourself a future.
>
> Plant deep in heart and mind
> In faithful hope these seeds of song
> If your poets are dear to you,
> So that from them a Springtime, a new one,
> Will grow. —What then remained of fire,
> Let it enflame you to the deed![13]

This is a more compressed version of what is found in the narratives: here, as there, the Czech endeavors to achieve autonomy are recognized as entirely legitimate; here, also, is a warning against all-too-radical apostles of freedom; and here, too, salvation follows automatically from poetic immersion in an apolitical, inner world. The coming victory is once again clothed in the metaphor of a self-regenerative spring. To be sure, many pressing questions remain unanswered. What sort of "new springtime" is it that will rise up out of song? What sort of "deed" is it that Rilke claims the poetically spiritualized people will be capable of? What distinguishes this deed from the program of the adamantly rejected poets of strife?

Certainly it would be wasted labor to puzzle out hidden meanings behind this amateurish effort at poetry. It is quite unlikely that the youthful René really thought through the various political alternatives. What is important for our inquiry is to note the presence, even at this early stage, of a characteristic attitudinal duality: on the one hand, Rilke's rejection, as a matter of principle, of violent changes in the social order as it is guaranteed by law, and on the other hand, his sympathy for the Czech people and for the creation of a national identity out of the people's own initiative and efforts, no matter how vaguely these might be characterized.

Viewed in terms of the predominant tendencies of the nineteenth century and subsequent historical developments, this rather automatic, insufficiently motivated triumph of the Czech people—really the stylized embodiment of a universal humanity—can be thought of as representing a "progressive" position. In the ever-sharpening conflict between the two peoples, the young Rilke chose the side opposed to his own national group. Indeed, his appraisal of which elements were moribund and which emergent was to be proven correct by future events.[14] This is the "progressive" aspect of his early works. But there are also present here—less apparently perhaps, but no less recognizably—"reactionary" traits, reactionary in the sense of adherence to the status quo and resistance to forces of change. On the periphery of the narrated action, and in a manner that thoroughly corresponds to the historical facts, Rilke's stories capture the Czech movement both in its national and social impulses. Even the term "democratic" appears. And since this insight regarding the social dimensions of the movement is attributed to the satirized von Meerings, one could even suspect that the young author—through a kind of narrative indirection—declares his solidarity with the egalitarian tendencies of Czech nationalism. For this reason it is advisable to point out the narrow limits that are set for this playful identification with political rebellion.

Consider, for example, the character Bohusch. A new insight separates him from the Czech activists with whom, like the figures from "The Siblings," he associates himself on account of his Slavic origins. Previously he had believed "that the wealthy and advantaged were, so to speak, allies

of destiny, which acts like an enemy only to poor devils."
The change of view is not exactly earthshaking. Few revolutionaries, like Bohusch, have been detained in their incendiary plans by the realization that even society's privileged are not protected from every form of human misery. But in his case this very recognition carries enormous consequences: "A whole bundle of prejudices fell all of a sudden from his hands," we are informed, "and something akin to a world view, a religion, was granted him."[15] This is a strong statement, and we have reason to believe that Rilke projected a good deal of himself into the figure of the imaginative hunchback.[16] But nowhere is the identification of author and character more plausible than at this crossroads of their development. The end of the tale, where the student Rezek strangles to death the dreamer Bohusch because of his alleged betrayal of the cause, alludes to historical events.[17] In contrast to what actually took place, however, the murder victim in the narrative is innocent of the transgressions he is accused of. Nevertheless, he suffers—at least from the standpoint of the nationalists—a sort of poetic justice, for he had long since defected in his heart from the liberation movement. In their eventual dissociation from the concrete social goals of Czech nationalism, Bohusch (in "King Bohusch") and Luisa (in "The Siblings") reflect Rilke's own development into an apolitical man.

A similar attitude informs the *Stories of Our Dear Lord*, which were written soon after.[18] "It was at the time when people were fighting for their freedom in southern Russia," the first-person narrator begins "The Song of Justice." But he is immediately interrupted by his soul brother Ewald, not coincidentally another cripple, who bursts forth with the following, highly revealing flow of words: "Pardon me, . . . what does that mean—did the people want to separate itself from the czar? That doesn't fit with the way I imagine Russia, nor with your other tales.[19] This time I'd rather not listen to your story. I love the image that I've

EARLY IMPRESSIONS

formed of life there and would just as soon keep it unspoiled."[20]

A remarkable view of history this, which declares itself ready to ignore whatever facts might contradict it! And the answer with which Ewald's worries are dispelled is so central for Rilke's emerging view of history, anticipates so exactly the world view of the broad middle class which comes to feel increasingly threatened by modernity, that we will do well to pay it the strictest attention: "I smiled and consoled him," the narrator continues. "The Polish Pans—I should have mentioned this before—were the masters in southern Russia and in those still and lonely steppes that are called the Ukraine. *They were hard masters. The oppression they exercised along with the greed of the Jews*, who even held the key to the church and would only turn it over to the faithful if given payment—these things had made the young people around Kiev and along the Dnjepr tired and reflective."[21]

The phrase, "I consoled him," in the introductory sentence contains a political avowal which, if one also considers the story's title, amounts to this: social injustice is not caused by aspects of the inner structure of society and cannot for that reason be eliminated through revolution; rather it is to be attributed to influences that come from outside, to exploitation perpetrated by foreign conquerors and the profit-hungry Jews allied with them who conduct their business unperturbed, even by the most sacred of customs. The antidote to these ills is a popular uprising with the aim of shaking off the foreign hegemony and escaping the grip of the Jewish parasites. That justice will be restored in this way is a fact that requires no demonstration but rather is tacitly presupposed. Rilke's story ends with the armed peasants marching off to battle; the outcome is left to the reader's imagination which has been primed for the task by several historical allusions. This prescription, the main ingredients of which are a frenzied national will and an anti-

Semitism composed of both economic and religious elements, would be applied throughout central Europe during Rilke's lifetime and soon after his death would cover half the globe with its nefarious power. The negative impression this passage makes is mitigated somewhat by the fact that Rilke borrowed the story from another work, Alfred Rambaud's *La Russie Epique*.[22] There we find the following passages, which clearly prefigure Rilke's text: "The enemy will no longer be the Turk or the Tartar but the Polish Pan or the Polishized Russian along with his two acolytes, the Catholic missionary and the Jewish bailiff or rental agent who will rent out everything in the Ukraine, the roads and the taverns, the fields and the streams, the statutes and the royalties—even the keys to the church where you will no longer be baptized, married, or mourned except with his permission." Or: "It will be Bogdan Khmelniçki, the advocate of the war of independence, who will give the signal to do battle against this unpopular trinity: the master, the Jesuit, the Jewish leaseholder." It is interesting that Rilke makes a duality out of this "trinity" and exempts the Catholic missionary from the accusation. Despite the fact that one subscribes to opinions borrowed in this way, artistic freedom asserts itself in the omissions and emendations.

In the following story from the collection, "A Scene from the Venice Ghetto," Rilke sketches the figure of another Jew, the patriarch Melchisedech, but this time with the traits of a venerable seer of God. As if he wanted to disprove what he had previously said, he writes here: "As soon as trouble came over the nation revenge was taken on the Jews."[23] The old Melchisedech, in addition, is an apolitical man. Upon hearing the report "that a rebellion had broken out in Venice, that the nobility was in danger and soon the borders of the ghetto would fall," the old man says nothing but continues his inner search for God undisturbed by such prospects. Rilke's attitude toward the Jews will be treated more fully in a later section.

EARLY IMPRESSIONS

In these stories we likewise find the beginnings of Rilke's increasingly intense concern with those problems he subsumed under the concept of "poverty." By this term Rilke understood a good deal more than material need. It designated for him a whole series of social ills, from the severance of traditional communal bonds, to sickness and the plight of invalids, to the spiritual misery of the individual in the huge modern cities. So persistently did he attempt from work to work to understand, to explain, even to accord a value to these phenomena, that one would be justified in speaking of a sort of theodicy. Without anticipating too much the insights into human misery that characterize his mature works, one can already say on the basis of the youthful works alone that for Rilke poverty is willed by God. This, at least, is the unmistakable implication of the story title, "Why Our Dear Lord Wants There to Be Poor People."[24] As another, somewhat later and more famous statement would have it, "Poverty is a great shining forth from within,"[25] that is to say, a privileged state of the soul. This idea appears throughout Rilke's early work in a variety of guises, perhaps most impressively in one of the *Stories of Our Dear Lord* entitled "The Begger and the Proud Young Lady." There the feelings of the benevolent Beatrice Altichieri are described in a manner that certainly applies as well to Rilke himself: ". . . it never occurred to her that there could be *strange* beggars; how could one ever attain the right to give them something since one had not earned the trust and intimacy of their poverty through intuition? Wouldn't it have been an unheard of presumption to grant alms to a stranger?"[26] Both sides then, the suffering *and* the alleviation of poverty, are private rather than public matters and can be understood only from the spiritual positions of those who give and those who receive the alms.

Such an extremely individualistic notion of poverty is of course not Rilke's property alone, but rather an age-old component of Christian doctrine. Nor is this correspondence an isolated case: Rilke's thought is so suffused with Christian elements—sometimes adopted unchanged, sometimes modified in a most idiosyncratic manner—that one is justified in speaking of him as a post-Christian poet (since he categorically renounced Christianity). However, in the context of the social world view that he begins to construct in Prague, the classification of poverty as a phenomenon of inner life serves a rather transparent function: since the ills of the community do not have their source in the existing social order and therefore have no external causes—unless, of course, it is a matter of repression on the part of a foreign power, in which case a liberation movement is allowable—they can therefore not be eliminated through external means but only through a deep-reaching purification of man. Poverty is an indispensable aid in the achievement of this higher humanity. What we have here is a Christian equivalent of the Marxist theory of the fully expropriated class; both have been disproved by empirical historical experience.

Now we can better understand what compelled the removal of the rebel Zdenko from the scene of "The Siblings," and what was behind the "automatic," that is to say, apolitical, triumph of his sister Luisa, a triumph justified by nothing more than by her higher humanity. This girl, allied as she is with a burgeoning nature and the inevitable coming of spring, emerges as fully superior vis-à-vis the outmoded foreign forces of domination, a fact pantomimically demonstrated in her victorious scene with the wife of Colonel Meering. It is not without interest to note that Rilke has once again appropriated for himself certain age-old notions regarding national character: the spontaneous depth of soul of the Slavs as opposed to the rationalistic, rigidly conventional Germans. Demetz argues that Rilke has adopted here a view traditionally held by Germans from the eastern reaches of the Empire, a view which represents the Czechs as a young and naïve people, not actually slaves in a political sense but rather immature children not fully recognized nor qualified with an hereditary title.[27] Much in the *Two Stories of Prague* confirms this and, of course, Rilke was in no way free of the opinions current in his environment. In view of Luisa's apotheosis in "The Siblings," however, this must be given a somewhat more positive accent, especially since it precedes the journey to Russia! Indeed, one gains a sense of the genuinely warm feelings for the Czechs with which Rilke infused even common clichés from the following notice for the *Two Stories of Prague* that he wrote in Petersburg in 1899: "Dreamy and sad are these human beings who so seldom act. Slavic yearning is in their voices and they live from the matinal piety of their natural feelings. And then there's a new element as well: the story of a people's childhood. A few words suggest, almost in passing, the destiny of a people who can't let their childhood grow and flower next to the older, more earnest and mature brother-race."[28] In any case, the cause of Rilke's lifelong rejection of every form of Teutonism is to be sought in this early phase, along with the sources of that complex sensibility that fed his countless expressions of cosmopolitan attachments:

> In order to understand how hard these historical developments are on me you must recall that I don't feel and sense things in a "German" way—not at all; although I cannot be entirely estranged from what is German, since I am spread out in the language all the way to the roots, its present actualization and its current belligerent consciousness have, as far as I can recall, provided me nothing but astonishment and irritation; and to make a home in Austria is for me unthinkable and unimaginable! How can I—I who was formed and educated by Russia, France, Italy, Spain, the desert and the Bible—how can I possibly find harmony among those who boast and swagger so around me![29]

This is the lament of the poet decades later when he is about to be called up for military service for the sake of the honor and glory of the fatherland. Among those powers he names as his educators, he surely could have named his native Bohemia first.

Looking back, Rilke interpreted his youth as rebellious or, to be more exact, as standing under the sign of "contradiction," of "resistance and liberation." We place these expressions within quotation marks because of a letter written in 1922, one of those rare retrospective views in which a human being attempts to grasp, from the distance of maturity, the conditions of his own development. A statement of this sort is especially well suited to confirm or to contradict the speculations of literary critics. We therefore cite it *in extenso*:

> In my youth . . . things were quite simply such that I had to get away, even at the risk of offending or hurting people. I cannot relate to you the Austrian situation of those days, a situation which must have been so without prospects and so moribund that my instinct told me: to grow naturally outward, to grow into those circumstances that life apparently held in store for me, would be an absolutely impossible undertaking even for the most combative of powers . . . and yet, if you ask me, I would not want *this* to be the impression that emanates from these works: not the call to some rebellion or liberation, not a leaping away from surroundings that make their demands on one, this is not—I would wish—what young people would adduce from these writings; rather, I would want them, in a new conciliatory spirit, to accept the given, the exacted, in some circumstances the necessary; not to flee from all this by going away, but by taking refuge in something deeper; not so much to resist the pressures of the situation as to exploit them in order to be placed thereby into a denser, deeper, more authentically self-related level of their own nature.[30]

Here we find united all the elements thus far taken note of in the early works. Each of the traits we have described corresponds to something mentioned in this letter. The con-

EARLY IMPRESSIONS

ciliatory spirit of acceptance that the mature poet here urges upon the younger generation is, however, not nearly as new as he believes. It had been preached by him for a long time, just as rebellion and liberation had been also.

We are now in a position to formulate an overall judgment of this phase of Rilke's development, a phase that will prove to be of extreme importance for everything that is to follow. The son of parents acutely dissatisfied with their social position, the sensitive young man reacted with a sharply critical attitude toward the social class to which he and his family belonged, the German minority in Bohemia. As a defense against threats to its privileges this group had enclosed itself in an unapproachable rigidity and intolerance. One must also recall that the Germans were perceived by Rilke as the representatives and beneficiaries of the Austrian state, which thereby met with his rejection as well. The decisive factor in this total rejection of his own social milieu, however, was probably Rilke's experience in the military academies. This attempt to afford him access into the higher social spheres failed because of his psychological constitution. Equipped by his mother with fantasy, religious mysticism, spiritual inclination, and youthful poetic ambition, Rilke was gradually worn down by the sober atmosphere of these imperial schools so averse to every intellectual and artistic endeavor. The unremittingly bitter outbursts regarding this time as a cadet—even as much as thirty years afterwards—are well known. After such an experience, the only way out for this young person, who painfully felt the inner demands of abilities that could not be developed in the atmosphere of his home, was a "liberation," although for the time being he could not determine what direction this would take. The Czechs, who were fighting to throw off an oppression, albeit a socio-political one, could hardly have played a role for Rilke in all this. After all, he wasn't one himself and nationality is exclusive. Nevertheless, their destiny, so similar to his own, served him temporarily as a vehicle to mirror poetically his own predicament. The *Two Stories of Prague* of 1897, which have served as our main illustrations, already appeared to their author when they went to press in 1899 as "nothing but the past."[31] For that reason, Rilke is entirely justified when he says in the foreword to his book: "Today I wouldn't have written it *this way*, and for that reason probably wouldn't have written it at all. But, at the time I wrote it, it was absolutely necessary for me." What allied Rilke with the Czechs was the impulse directed against the German mandarin class representing the Austrian state. What separated him from the Czechs was the social-revolutionary element in their national movement from which he, as a German, remained excluded anyway. Rilke felt his freedom threatened by the ossified ruling class whose privileges he could share in only by virtue of psychological concessions that were impossible for him to make. At the same time, his development as an elitist poet was threatened by the democratic demands of the masses. For this reason, all real, social problems are transposed, within the concept of "poverty," into phenomena of the inner life. The two central figures of the *Two Stories of Prague*, the cripple Bohusch and the sensitive maiden Luisa, both of whom dwell in a fantasy world, are, by virtue of their function, no longer Czechs but reflexes of René Rilke. Their renunciation of their political rights corresponds to the "conciliatory spirit," their inner life to the "something deeper" of the letter quoted above where the term "moribund" refers to the German-Austrian milieu. Although still in a primitive form, we find in this letter most of the material out of which Rilke's subsequent social views will be composed and which made possible his no longer so surprising partisanship for Italian fascism. The dissatisfaction with the prevailing social conditions, the yearning for a radical liberation—this coupled with the disavowal of truly effective changes in the social structure, the romantic transfiguration of nature and of life in the provinces, the

EARLY IMPRESSIONS

enmity toward the modern city with its characteristic undermining of traditional morals and its proletarianization of the petite bourgeoisie, the transposition of concrete social problems into a sublimated internal realm, the positing of national conflicts, and finally the denial of the conflict between the individual classes—these are all typical attitudes of the conservative movement, which was supported by the middle classes and which, as most social scientists agree, led to fascism even if fascism eventually betrayed their hopes to the capitalist industrialism that these groups so hated.

Chapter 3
World War

The years following his departure from Prague were immensely significant for Rilke. Although quite well known, several of the most important factors in the poet's development should be mentioned here. Above all, Rilke's friendship with Lou Andreas-Salomé had an inestimable effect on the poet's career. Anyone who might be led astray by certain negative interpretations of this relationship[1] need only ask what would otherwise have become of this provincial autodidact so uncertain of his own taste, indeed of his own value. For the first time in his life the poet was fully accepted by a truly important person, admitted not only into that person's intimate sphere but also into the highest strata of contemporary cultural life. And here we have the second decisive factor in the young man's development: through this woman and her circle, Rilke had access to that grand world—culturally and socially speaking—in which he would henceforth move and for which his artistic production was intended. The third gift for which Rilke had Lou to thank, and which would prove so essential for his life, was travel—especially the trip to Italy and the two journeys to Russia that Rilke undertook under her influence and, in part, in her company. Only after his separation from Lou did Rilke embark upon an independent, self-determined course of life; important signposts were to follow: Worpswede and marriage, Paris with Rodin and Cézanne, the many journeys back and forth across half the world, from Scandinavia to Egypt and Spain. During almost two decades, from 1896 to 1914, Rilke acquired—despite the impression given by conventional biographies—a good deal of socio-historical experience. In Russia he became acquainted with an agrarian society to his liking, in Paris with the oppressive and yet fascinating phenomenon of a modern city, a metropolis produced by an industrial state.

But all that took place, as it were, in a subterranean manner. Along with many great (and small) minds of his epoch, Rilke dedicated his most intensive intellectual energies during this relatively untroubled time prior to World War I to the acquisition and expansion of his artistic self-conception. Unable to embrace either of the communities that were available to him in his youth, the Czech and the German, he withdrew into an extreme aestheticizing individualism. Going beyond the principle of *l'art pour l'art*, he postulates an art that exists solely for the sake of the artist: "Know, then, that art is this: the means through which singular, solitary individuals fulfill themselves."[2] It has been rightly argued that the educational trip to Italy Rilke undertook in 1898 provided the basis for this notion of art.[3] The *Florentine Diary* that Rilke wrote for the distant Lou teems with manifesto-like statements whose goal is self-isolation from every possible community.

In the *Diary* it is said that the people actually don't want art,[4] indeed that they hate works of art.[5] Art supposedly traces an arc from individual to individual above the heads of the people.[6] The artist is in truth a creature born of estrangement: "He has his home nowhere except with himself."[7] When Rilke, himself the author of several dramas, writes: "The drama is so undignified precisely because it requires a public,"⁸ one hears not only Stefan George but the consensus of all the asocial, elitist writers of the age who attempted to flee from a society and culture in dissolution into a new religion of art. For that reason, it is not so much the content of such formulations that is revealing as the way they are expressed, for here we can recognize the individual nuances of a world view. What is striking, for example, in a statement like the following is the implication that for Rilke this forced aestheticism is associated with a radical denial of history: "Protect art so that it experiences nothing of the disputes of the day, its home is outside all time."⁹ Is stronger evidence required to show that this apolitical man's antagonistic attitude toward "the disputes of the day" presupposes a political position, and not at all an innocent one? We are in a position to bring such evidence forward.

"Imagine Michelangelo being discussed in some newspaper," the youthful opponent of the press speculates, "regardless of whether he's praised or attacked—with those clichés of Jewish nit-picking that have grown shiny from use. I think he would have pounded the critic into shape like a miscarved block of marble."¹⁰ The combination of aestheticizing snobbism, anti-Semitic pseudo-wit, and vulgar brutality found here points to an all-too-familiar complex, which, unfortunately, was to enjoy a dynamic future.

Not that such a world view can be maintained without internal challenge. Indeed, what are Malte's much pondered crises of the soul but desperate attempts to defend this world view against the onslaught of social and historical reality? In the main, however, the poet's outlook remains unchanged till the end of his life. Only once, during the First World War, do concrete historical forces, the demands of the day, break into his consciousness with such vehemence that they cannot be denied. Incapable of retreating completely from the convulsions of a tortured humanity, Rilke turns his attention consciously and deliberately to matters of social exigency. From the details of this intellectual activity we can gain new insights into Rilke's entanglement with the historical conditions of his age.

Like his childhood sufferings, Rilke's torment during the World War has not gone unnoticed by the commentators.[11] And yet we cannot avoid taking up the matter again from our particular perspective. Whoever recalls the passage cited above, "I don't feel and sense things in a German way . . ."[12] will not expect any sort of war enthusiasm from Rilke. Nevertheless, caught by surprise in Germany at the outbreak of the war, the poet was, if not seized, at least touched by the nationalist intoxication. And whatever the extent of his inner participation, the poet did in fact celebrate the god of war in his *Five Songs*,[13] written in Munich on the second and third of August, 1914. Really celebrated? A look at the formulations these poems contain will soon convince us that it is unjust to accuse Rilke of *enthusiasm* for war.

"Finally a god." This exclamation from the first song illuminates most adequately the psychological motivation of the entire poem-cycle. Out of the uncertainty (now we see that it was uncertainty!) of peacetime intellectual disorientation something unquestionable and relentless rises up, something before which every individual, including the total outsider, must yield, every sceptical stance capitulate. Among all the figures gripped by the war with whom Rilke seeks to empathize in the first song, the young man is doubtless the closest to him:

> . . . . him, who just a while ago
> perceived a hundred voices, not knowing which was in the
>   right,
> how this one call now relieves him; for *what* would not be
> sheer whim next to joyful, next to secure exigency?

A similar feeling of relieved self-sacrifice, of being carried along by the stream of the masses, would years later push not a few human beings into the European fascist movements.

The sense of absorption in a general intoxication then becomes the central theme of the second song: "Happy am I who sees men stirred." This formulation points to the fact that it is the turbulent psychological state and not the external cause that is of importance here. And, to be sure, we find that calling forth of the archaic so characteristic of the intellectual forced into isolation by the fragmentation of modernity (to employ for a change a term other than the hackneyed "alienated man"): the "maidens of pre-time," the primitive "feeling of fathers," the anachronistic "mountain of heroes." Suddenly one is reminded of Gottfried Benn's "laboriously sustained" and finally abandoned "rationalism."[14]

In the third song the deindividualizing tumult spills over onto the poetic 'I':

> So I too *am* no longer; from a common heart
> my heart takes its beat, and a common mouth
> breaks my mouth open.

The solitary singer has once again become the voice of the popular soul. But already the first sobering reflection is registered in this third song and uncertainties impose themselves on poet and reader alike: "Do I really praise the terror?" the speaker asks in disbelief. Despite all his yearning for self-surrender and sacrifice, he knows: "Nevertheless, there howls in me . . . a questioning something." This scepticism refuses to be suppressed and so rejection and affirmation wrestle with one another even in these allegedly enthusiastic poems. What attracts the poet is the "holy communal,"[15] what makes him hesitate is the tribute this communal feeling demands—the sacrifice of his individual

WORLD WAR

reason:

> Can
> he be one who knows, this ripping God?
> For indeed he destroys everything known. That which so
>   long and so loving,
> which so familiarly we have known.[16]

The remainder of the cycle is dedicated to sorrow. The recrudescence of archaic feelings is renounced, the experience of the war affirmed, to be sure, but that element of the war that robs one's individuality is countered through a dialectical trick. "Imitate not what was earlier,"[17] is the warning given. Out of the primitive "battle-lust" there should develop a "battle-sorrow" which purifies and internally refines the individual. This reversal is already quite familiar to us: as in the case of poverty, a general evil along with all its social causes is overcome by dissociating it from all real circumstances and internalizing it. Man can draw individualistic advantages even from the barbaric regressions of the fighting and the severing of all bonds between peoples:

> For to understand,
> for to learn and to hold much in honor
> within, even foreign things, that was the calling you felt,
> now you are restricted again to what's yours.
> And yet it's
> become greater. Even if it isn't the world, not by far—
> take it as the world![18]

However one interprets these songs, one thing must not be forgotten: they are, in the final analysis, a recognition of the fact of war and its elemental power much more than an enthusiastic glorification and justification such as we find among several of Rilke's contemporaries, and not the most insignificant ones at that. Rilke's intoxication—if indeed it was such and not merely the wish of the single sober man among drinkers to enjoy a moment of intoxication—was brief. The sobering-up, however, lasts the entire war. From now on, his statements about the event—which gradually developed into an ongoing state of affairs—are a never-ending litany of lament. Still during the month of August, he confesses his error with an appealing openness and precision of self-scrutiny: "For the first few days my spirit moved along in the great, general stream and was able in its way to participate; but then I reflected on myself as an inexpressibly solitary individual, reflected on my old, past heart (which I cannot abandon), and now I have a very hard time of it as I bend over these pages and attempt, entirely alone, to come to a legitimate position vis-à-vis the monstrous general state of things. Fortunate are those who are inside of it, whom it carries along, whose voices it swallows up."[19] And alluding unmistakably to the *Songs* (first published in 1951), he acknowledges: ". . . for a long time now the war has become invisible to me, a spirit of persecution, no longer a god but the unleashing of a god among the peoples."[20] This is the way it remains. And so one can count Rilke among the earliest and most uncompromising opponents of the First World War.

There would be little point in quoting here the manifold jeremiads, produced out of a thousand different occasions, formulated in a thousand different ways, and yet saying again and again the same thing: "the evil,"[21] "the horror,"[22] "nothing but wretchedness,"[23] "the nameless human doom."[24] These expressions are merely a modest selection from the vocabulary that Rilke musters up over the next four years in order to convey to his many correspondents his horror at the war. Who would deny that these outbursts had to do, as always, with his own poetic production? Indeed, Rilke had always suffered severely from recurrent periods of sterility, whatever their cause might have been, and he was only happy when productive. For that reason, a clever observer several years ago compared Goethe, the creator out of overabundance, with Rilke, the creator out of lack, thereby reversing Goethe's statement that "one has to be something in order to make something," in order to apply it to Rilke: "One must make something in order to be something."[25] The most eloquent testimony of this paralysis is to be found in a letter written two years before the war's end: "It's true that this persistence of the world in such incomprehensible wickedness creates for my nature, which can only move in the absence of wickedness, a state of total paralysis, but ought not, I say to myself, this limitless exigency, that comes to awareness in me more forcefully than in others, ought not it extort from me an activity, sorrowful words or helpful ones, or a single, great word, a scream? Nothing of the kind. The longer the horrible emergency and destruction lasts, the more I feel myself grow stiff."[26] Nowhere is his helplessness during the war more movingly perceptible than in those passages where, instead of speaking directly of his poetic muteness, he alludes in a brief sentence or an aside to the total exhaustion of his expressive powers. Such is the case, for example, in a letter where he describes the Chiemsee (a lake south of Munich) in order, then, to add, in a fit of pusillanimity apparently become habitual, the following: "I doubt whether in these lines the individual things I've seen struggle their way through to become an actual image. It is as if the ravaged age prevented me from achieving an appropriate synthesis in myself."[27]

If this were all, then it would differ little from earlier episodes of despair when Rilke could only deal with the world and its destinies by viewing it as material for his own poetic production. In that case one could not speak of the World War as a decisive event intervening in his spiritual existence. But such an exceptional phenomenon as this murder of entire peoples could not be perpetually overlooked for what it was even by a Rilke. With increasing frequency new tones are absorbed into his lamentations; with increasing regularity his thoughts seem to digress from his own distress to the universal situation of need so that gradually his entire consciousness is brought into play and practically reverses itself. At the age of forty, of course, one cannot simply leap out of deeply ingrained patterns of thought. As we observed with regard to his notion of poverty, the internalization of external reality is for Rilke programmatic, almost a compulsion. Thus there is no dearth of attempts to fabricate an internal significance for the war as well. The war should have been, he suggests, "a real raging," something "truly splendid."[28] But the senselessness of the butchery proves too astonishingly evident, the personal losses too terrible, the nation, for whose glory all this might have been justified, becomes too estranged from the poet for him to consider for long such an explanation. The necessary first step to a realistic appraisal is a demythologizing one: "I would forbid myself all lamenting," so he ruminates, "if the general fate were of the nature of a more divine destiny; but it seems to me, as I look about for such signs, that there is nothing but what is of human making, human error, intolerance, greed, humanest obstinancy."[29] Coming from someone who lives in a universe moved by metaphysical powers, this is a heroic confession. The next step is to search for a scapegoat who can be blamed for the meaningless dispersion of all the wondrous stirrings of the soul. The press, which for a long time had seemed suspect to him and in which the nationalistic mendacity was most densely concentrated, offered a convenient target for his wrathful accusations. We need only recall here the brilliant invectives of a Karl Kraus, the implacable critic of contemporary journalism, in order to see how unoriginal was Rilke's thinking in these matters. Quite often in his letters now we hear about "the loathsome press, which certainly bears much of the guilt for this war and still more guilt for the fact that ambiguity and falsification have made a disease" of the beautiful possibilities for an internal appropriation of the suffering. The press is also blamed for the fact that "everything that was of the nature of sacrifice and decisiveness has been lumped together in a heap of miserable and untrue statements." Then an entirely new element enters into the calculation: "*swallowed up by the 'enterprise' of this war, the purpose of which is to make profit.*"[30] This can no longer be regarded as an attempt to subordinate the events of the external world to his own artistic project or even to integrate them within it. An anticapitalist protest of this nature—no matter how simplistic—must be evaluated as an element within a new view of society, as a new turn in Rilke's path through the concrete world of cause and effect which this book endeavors to trace out.

When compelled to come to terms with the war, Rilke begins to expand, modify, and correct his earlier views. The sincerity of his efforts is underlined by the fact that he does not recoil from overturning even his most privately treasured ideas and patches up things he had believed in axiomatically: "I sense only now to what degree all my feeling and creativity—even given all my exclusivity—was based on the silent presupposition that it proceeded in a world similarly oriented, similarly striving."[31] The aesthete who thought himself entirely self-sufficient discovers that what seemed to be the most solitary productions are dependent on a community, a silently presupposed social contemporaneity: "For no matter how solitary and exclusive one might have been, a certain secure understanding was in the end the unacknowledged presupposition of every creation and every joy."[32]

From this insight it is only a step to calling his earlier aesthetics and mode of production into doubt. "Can that in any way diminish the pain over the fact that such confusion, such not-knowing-where-to-turn . . . was necessary in order to extort demonstrations of courage, sacrifice and greatness?"[33] In the new context this can only be a rhetorical question to which the answer must be an unequivocal "no." We are dealing here with yet another surprising concession: namely, that it will not suffice to console ourselves about anything and everything that happens in the world simply by evaluating it as a stimulus to handsome deeds and feelings, that is to say aesthetically. Likewise, it would be logically consistent for Rilke to diverge from the solipsism that had characterized the earlier practice of his poetic vocation. He in no way refuses to draw this conclusion. Instead, he continues his line of thought with admirable logical rigor: "Meanwhile we, the arts, the theater, called forth in these same human beings nothing at all, we brought nothing to its ascent, were able to transform no one. What else is our métier except to present purely and grandly and freely causes for change—have we done that so badly, so half-way, so unconvincingly?"[34] Coming from Rainer Maria Rilke, these are significant sentences. Has an Enlightenment impulse asserted itself here? Is the purpose of art to "improve and convert?" Are the changes that art calls forth perhaps too slow? Was the earlier artistic practice wrong? Could the function of poetry be to educate man, to give him aid for the tasks of life? The implications that follow from an epistolary statement such as that just cited lead far way from the existential-artistic project of the Florence diary;[35] from such implications to a new interest in direct social action is only a short leap of thought.

One must understand this development of Rilke's as neither irrevocable nor linear. It was not a chronologically chartable casting-off of old habits of thought now recognized as false as my narrative has perhaps suggested. It is better conceived as a wavering, an exploration, a retraction, a realignment, and then a renewed push forward. Finally, however, he wrestles his way through to a scream of protest which, without this preparation, would necessarily remain incomprehensible and which, removed entirely from context, would hardly be attributable to a Rilke: "Can no one hinder it and hold it back? Why aren't there a few, three, five, ten, who stand together on the plazas and scream: enough! and get shot down and at least give their lives that it might be known it's gone far enough, while those outside die only so that the terror continues and there's no end in sight for the dying."[36] The passage continues and it is noteworthy with what passion Rilke develops the thought and yearns for a community of resisters: "Why is there not just *one* person, who no longer bears it, *can* no longer bear it? If he only would cry out a single night through in the false city hung with flags, cry out and not let himself be silenced, who could call him for that reason a liar? How many hold back with effort this scream—or not? If I am in error and there are not many who could scream so, then I don't understand men, am not one and have nothing in common with them."[37] In this passage one can also see how central to Rilke's social views is the expressed or stifled protest. The idea of resisting a social event—of resisting it through group action—is definitively new. How very new it is can be measured if one compares it to the demand for an unconditional enduring and waiting such as can be found in the *Stories of our Dear Lord*.[38] Beyond this, one should be fully prepared for the most peculiar and most unrilkean "inclination to the left" which he expressed near the end of the war. "What sort of confusion will there be afterwards when all the notions accepted in full belief are taken down from the pedestals on which they had been set up. . . ?"[39] When that actually happened, Rilke was not at all shocked.

Almost more surprising than the repeatedly expressed acceptance of the idea of a revolution is the style of participation to which the once-so-exclusive aesthete accommodates himself. He takes note of announcements, reads the daily papers, follows events by the hour, attends speeches, lectures and other sorts of gatherings in the public rooms of beer halls. Rilke is impressed not merely by the academic experts who speak out on the question of peace, such as Max Weber, but still more by the voices of the people who cry for peace in a much more elemental way. It is moving that the lonely poet not only does not take offense at the physical aspect of these mass meetings but even finds complimentary words to describe them:

> And although people were sitting at and around the tables in such a way that the waitresses had to eat their way through the dense human structure like worms through wood, the atmosphere was not at all oppressive, it wasn't even hard to breathe; the aroma of beer and smoke and people was not unpleasant to take in; one hardly noticed it, so very important and presently clear to everyone was the fact that the things which were finally due could be said, and that the simplest and most valid of these things, as long as it was professed somewhat audibly, would be grasped by the immense crowd with heavy, massive applause.[40] "Such moments are wonderful,"[41] he acclaims.

Let us stay for another moment with this democratic Rilke, for he goes further than such enjoyment of the brotherhood of man. Revolution is affirmed in principle, indeed even in practice. He speaks approvingly of the Munich "Soldiers', Peasants' and Workers' Council" under Eisner,[42] whom he knows personally and acknowledges:

> As far as I'm concerned, there predominates in me, despite all worrisome care, an expansive confidence that reaches beyond this most pressing present, a feeling such as I have never known as regards the phenomenon of the war. Only now have authentic ideals become clear, most humane and inspiring ones, and we must not be led astray by the fact that the crowd stands up for them in such a heavy-headed and clumsy and helpless manner; it knows no better.[43]

And, from a more critical perspective

> I admit that at first I was able to seize a certain rash and joyful confidence at the idea of a revolution, for as long as I have been able to think I have wished for nothing more urgently than that humanity might sometime be granted the power to open an entirely new page of the future on to which the entire sum of errors of the fateful past would not have to be transferred. The revolution seemed to me to be such a gifted moment.[44]

Despite all the veiled adjectives and similes, this is an interesting and, for Rilke, and entirely new sort of avowal.

To be sure, this enthusiasm, like that for the war, did not last very long. Rapidly Rilke runs the gamut from mild distance to decisive rejection. What are the reasons that he gives for this disenchantment and what might the deeper, real causes have been? That the revolution was attempted by a "contingent . . . and unenthusiastic minority," that there was "no youth and fiery conviction" in it—certainly these are claims that can be neither demonstrated nor accepted as valid objections. His views that "beneath the pretense of a great revolution . . . the old lack of conviction" was really at work, or that the new state of things was "just as little *true* as the calls that had summoned to war,"[45] would have more weight if one only knew what was meant by them. On several occasions the reproach of a "political dilettantism"[46] appears. It seems that what disturbed Rilke was that the revolution was made by people who "outside of their knowledge and area of competence sought after the universal and introduced experimentation where only the wisest and most carefully considered things ought to be allowed to take effect."[47] Whoever speaks in this manner does not really want a revolution.

We are brought to the same conclusion on the basis of another objection that Rilke expresses: "After the indescribable efforts and exigencies of the war a moment of security and rest would have been the most indispensable of all things; one cannot conceive how the exerted efforts of the field campaigns could now be followed by the enormous efforts that are constantly required." Or, as he had phrased it earlier: "Perhaps revolutions are only possible in full-blooded moments."[48] This is the first objective reason against a revolution that Rilke offers: the people are too weakened by the war to make a revolution. But this is equivalent to saying that there cannot be revolutions in general. In periods of social tranquility and unshaken prosperity, in any case, that is, in "full-blooded times," they are not to be expected. From all this we can conclude that despite a certain dissatisfaction with conditions as they were, Rilke could not decide in favor of a radical upheaval. The play of his thoughts is most clearly revealed in a definition that inadvertently escaped him during his intellectual confrontation with these issues: "By the way, I understand revolution to mean the overcoming of abuses for the sake of the most profound tradition."[49] Now we see more clearly what he means: a revolution for the sake of tradition is a conservative revolution. With all his repugnance for the press, the profits of war, the financial world, modern technology and whatever else might be imagined as "abuses" or "the sum of errors of the fateful past," Rilke yearns for an order that builds on old elements and does not break through to something new. And so his flirtation with the revolution ends with the newly strengthened resolution to retreat from this brief engagement into the apolitical and internal spheres: "My inclination is now more than ever to do what I really can, *entirely against the call of the age*."[50]

If one looks at Rilke's attitude toward the events of the war and the immediate postwar period, the image of a "progressive" emerges. Apart from a brief and internally contradictory identification with the general mood at the outbreak of the war, Rilke was an early and unrelenting opponent of the war, and he remained so. More than this. He took the historical events which so transcended the old individualism of the prewar world as an incitement to revise his previous thinking and to criticize his *l'art pour l'art* position. There begins to develop within his view of art something like a "social consciousness." Rilke's disgust for the war even causes him—against his instinctive inclinations—to consider the possibility of active resistance. Having gone this far, he musters sympathy for the first phases of the political upheavals at the war's end, indeed, even for the Munich Council Republic. In this he resembles the majority of the German Enlightenment writers of the eighteenth century who, fed up with the social conditions of the *ancien régime*, at first welcomed the French Revolution. Like them, however, Rilke very rapidly distances himself from the revolution as soon as it contradicts, in its concrete manifestations, his own habitual notions. All of this could be placed without difficulty within the framework of democratic liberalism.[51] Such, however, would be an overhasty conclusion. Political gatherings in beerhouse halls, after all, are a popular form of meeting but not necessarily—as we all recall—a democratic one.

If one surveys Rilke's intellectual development between 1914 and 1919 in view of his later inclination toward Italian fascism—a twist for which we have been prepared from the very beginning of this study—then a more expansive ideological landscape opens up, allowing one to judge less one-sidedly. The lessons that Rilke drew from the war and the immediate postwar period can then be evaluated as follows: He recognizes or at least suspects that man's transformation through art and intellect proceeds much too slowly to thwart cataclysms on the scale of a world war. He inclines, therefore, for the first time toward social action directed against those forces that allow such events to take place, perhaps even consciously unleash them. A letter to Anni Mewes, dated December 9, 1918, attacks the "intellect" with considerable scepticism: "Neither the latter nor the former [the postwar revolution and the call to war] were made by the intelligentsia. The so-called intelligentsia came to this event rather late and was only capable—exactly as in 1914—of 'making itself available,' which, one must concede, is not exactly spectacular on the part of the intelligentsia."[52] In Rilke's work, this is a fairly singular insight into the powerlessness of intellect in history. Something like a flash of comprehension that state, press, and society form a ruling elite, a systematic unity against which a revolutionary uprising from below is legitimate, characterizes his thinking. "The current atmosphere and state of mind denies me and refutes me in my inmost feelings . . . and yet it is so easy to place oneself among them [the population] that one wishes less than ever to be counted among the 'higher ones' but rather stands in suffering among the lowliest, poorer, more restricted than they, persecuted where possible by an even more pressing injustice."[53] In all this he is really developing—more than departing from—potential beginnings present since the time of his youth. We cannot adjust the facts: opposition to war and antichauvinism are in no way conducive to a later inclination toward fascism. What can be said is that Rilke's development runs parallel to that of certain "old conservative" circles into "conservative revolutionaries." It was a shift being prepared for throughout Europe, one which constituted a trend that lent a substantial amount of force to the fascist movements. Rilke is likewise similar to thinkers of this ilk in that he recoils before a radical revolution with all its consequences. To be sure, such hesitation is also psychologically conditioned. Rilke's quick infatuation—be it for a cause or for a person—and his almost immediately subsequent withdrawal have been often enough observed. Since we are not concerned here with Rilke's psychology we merely allude to this "behavior pattern" in passing. Instead, our final question must be formulated as follows: in view of his tendency to always return to his point of departure, to what degree did Rilke hold to the ideological shifts which the experience of the war had effected in him? There can be no doubt that he tried to retract them. Nevertheless the wheel of inner development could not be entirely turned back. Historical reality had penetrated his thinking and, in order to protect himself from it, he had to emphasize his enmity against the modern world ever more strongly, indeed ever more violently. In contrast to this, the period from approximately 1915 to 1919 will appear retrospectively as the phase in Rilke's development most open to the "humane" and the "social."

Chapter 4
Period of Maturity

The time has come for us to inquire what social theorists have to say regarding the ideological tendencies of the European Right. Despite the diversity of their origins and their aims, the older conservative movements and the social-conservative or conservative-revolutionary or fascist groups that sprang up after the First World War among certain sectors of the population in many countries exhibit far-reaching similarities. One is justified, therefore, in assuming that such inclinations are deeply rooted in the structure of Western society, especially when one considers the preparatory phase prior to the actual seizure of power by the fascist regimes.[1]

Researchers seem to be in agreement on one important point: fascism is to be viewed as a reaction to the twin phenomena of capitalism and the industrial revolution.[2] We can go one step further and add that the entire social and cultural history of recent times appears to be the sum of reactions to these and related developments such as secularization, democratization, and internationalism. It is a question here of long-term processes whose beginnings some researchers place in the eighteenth century, others as far back as the Renaissance and even the late Middle

PERIOD OF MATURITY 43

Ages. Only since the nineteenth century, however, have the mechanization, economization, and rationalization of all areas of life assumed such intensity that they cannot possibly be overlooked. This transformation of agrarian societies into industrial societies occurred nowhere without uprootings, hardship, and suffering—indeed, exploitation, brutality, and manifest injustice. Even in the Western countries, which were granted a relatively long period of adaptation, the process produced bad feelings, insecurity, and dissatisfaction among broad strata of the population. In certain parts of the continent, especially in Central Europe and in the Mediterranean countries where industrialism took hold late and therefore with real virulence, extremely intense conflicts were often the result. As Sauer writes: "It is perhaps not accidental that the industrialization process ran relatively smoothly in West European nations whose political rise concurred with the rise of modern civilization since the late Middle Ages. Fascist opposition was strongest in the Mediterranean and Central European regions where the premodern traditions of the ancient Roman and medieval German and Turkish Empires persisted."[3] Parsons likewise points to the fact that most Western countries changed in the course of the nineteenth and twentieth centuries from agricultural to industrial and commercial societies and that this had an immense influence on the life and activity of huge numbers of people.[4] An early literary treatment of the problem is to be found in the fifth act of *Faust II* where the collision of the idyllic, preindustrial way of life with technical civilization is mirrored in the conflict between Faust and Philemon and Baucis.

On the basis of my own studies and observations I have come to distinguish between three broad types of reaction to these transformations: first, the Left, which accepted technology and rationalization but rejected the social order in which these developments had arisen. Despite various sectarian departures from the basic doctrine, the goal of the Left remained the establishment of a socialist society where the accomplishments of modernity could be fully exploited and made accessible to all. This movement believed in international brotherhood and was based primarily in the working class and its ideologues, who mainly came from the middle class. Second, a middle position held by the great amorphous mass of those who tried to profit from the powerful process, sometimes resisting, usually yielding and supportive of industrialization. This position is characterized by a confusion of ideological variants, often by an even more alarming absence of thinking altogether. Its common denominator is expressed as a more or less successful adaptation to and acceptance of the unavoidable development. The third direction, the Right,[5] oriented itself primarily in terms of preindustrial and precapitalist models and demanded an inner renewal of man, on the basis of national tradition instead of a thoroughgoing reformation of the social structure. This direction was supported by those who were either threatened or harmed by the industrial revolution, which resulted in a broad social distribution of the Right that extended into the highest classes. For the most part, however, it was a question of the middle classes who were caught between the capitalists on the one side and the organized proletariat on the other.

> In the late nineteenth century and the early part of the twentieth the terrible abstractions of 'capital' and 'labor' came to loom over the middle classes, beckoning to them yet at the same time threatening to destroy them. Under conditions of great common hardship, as in the terrible twentieth-century depression, artisans, small shopkeepers, peasant proprietors, and white collar workers could find little guidance or comfort in the ideological blandishments of either big business or big labor.[6]

With all its diversity of interests, the Right is held together by its rejection of the capitalist economic system, of democratic massification, and in part of modern technology. It resists the scientific rationalism that is at the basis of all these systems by turning to irrationalist currents of the most diverse sorts. Psychologically, the bitter dissatisfaction with existing conditions gives the Right a certain unity. Moreover, as Sauer concludes: "Historical evidence shows that support of fascism may not be confined to the classical elements of the middle class (*Mittelstand*—peasants, artisans, small businessmen, and so forth), but may extend to a wide variety of groups in the large field between the workers on the one hand and big business, the aristocracy, and the top levels of bureaucracy on the other."[7]

Rilke belongs without question to the Right. As the descendant of a declining family and as an elitist artist, he must be identified with its aspirations. Of course, one must not imagine a highly individualized poet as totally fixed in his outlook, especially a Rilke who was constitutionally protected from every form of fanaticism by his hesitating temperament. It would be more apt to compare him with a highly sensitive recording instrument whose needle, to be sure, generally points in a certain direction but nevertheless remains in constant movement, always ready in the case of exceptional tremors to leap this way or that. Thus we have been able to observe, to take one example, that this needle could—during and immediately following the war—point quite far to the Left, even if only briefly and tentatively.[8]

Furthermore, we must recall that the harshest phase of fascism began only after Rilke's death with the consolidation of the Italian regime and the National Socialists' seizure of power in Germany. For the period of his lifetime one can only speak of a preparatory movement in which certain social-conservative tendencies are still hard to distinguish from genuine fascism. Such tendencies aided fascism in many respects, practically and ideologically, by removing the obstructions that stood in its path to absolute governmental power. For example, in Italy, which, as we have seen, Rilke favored with his sympathies, two stages of the development are usually distinguished: a first phase, during which the interests of the large agricultural landowners and the industrialists were protected, and, from 1925 on, a second phase in which an abrupt turn in financial and economic policy marked the transition from a relatively moderate coalition government to an ever more totalitarian regime.[9] Rilke probably perceived little of these latter displacements, but he was certainly aware of the support of fascism on the part of conservative groups and of Mussolini's declared support of the monarchy in 1922. In any case, he stood close enough to these circles that he could be requested to render his services at court.

On the distinction between a fascist regime and a prefascist movement, Sauer remarks: "There may be a marked difference between the original, relatively homogeneous fascist movements prior to the seizure of power and what emerges as fascist regimes after that event. This leads to the equally important problem of the relationships between fascist movements and their allies."[10] Significant, too, is the following sentence: "The *Action Française* is important . . . because Maurras succeeded in building an intellectual bridge between counterrevolutionary tradition and fascism. . ."[11] The literature on the subject too often fails to distinguish between the movements and the regimes. E. Weber is fully aware of this problem: "We have on the whole avoided discussion of the right-wing regimes that reached power. . . . When it becomes successful the extreme Right tends to turn into something else, which it is not our object to examine here."[12]

Although Rilke declared himself for the fascist *regime*, it is unlikely that he carefully followed or understood what had taken place in Italy during fascism's first phase. It is much more likely that he took the fascist gestures and propaganda at face value; this can be observed in his remarks in the *Lettres Milanaises*, which echo some of Mussolini's rhetorical flourishes. Besides, our present inquiry concerns a general ideology of the Right. For that reason we can say that there exist correspondences between Rilke and the *Action Française*, the German social conservatives and the German "folkish" groups, as well as the genuinely fascist movements of Germany and Italy.

The eventual destiny of the conservatives who, for a variety of reasons, promoted the cause of the fascists is not the object of this study.[13] Instead, we are concerned solely with certain inclinations that Rilke shared with a broad spectrum of the European Right. This also prevents us from making casual use of the technical term "fascism," which today has become a widely used pejorative label meaning every possible political phenomenon from "social fascism" to "clerical fascism."[14] There would be no value whatsoever in demonstrating that Rilke was a "fascist," a great deal of value, however, in recognizing those intellectual preconditions which contributed to his speaking so eloquently on behalf of Mussolini.

To be sure, the fact that Rilke belonged to the Right in this broadly conceived sense must first of all be securely established. This affinity emerges more clearly from his fundamental opposition to the existing order than from anything else. Rilke, in fact, stood in a relationship of intense and constant disagreement with the dominant cultural tendencies of his time. The only one to have pointed this out decisively—without drawing all the consequences from his observations—is the late English literary historian Eudo C. Mason:

> What misleads the critics . . . is the fallacious belief from which they set out, and for which Rilke himself must indeed largely be held responsible, that he is never in the opposition, that it is incompatible with his nature ever to resist or revolt against anything. It would be truer to say of him that

he is *always* in the opposition, though it remains a curiously disguised and therefore easily overlooked kind of underground opposition.[15]

Indeed, Rilke himself clearly recognized this opposition, and at the same time distinctly stated one of the central theses of this book: "*What I write artistically will probably always reveal the traces of the contradiction* by means of which I have positioned myself. . . ."[16] In an earlier letter he speaks of a "most intense and lasting rebellion"[17] because his father expected him to take up a career as an officer or a lawyer. The tension between external conformism and inner rebellion, coupled with a multiplicity of inclinations with which we shall soon become acquainted, determines Rilke's allegiance within the ideological tendencies of his century.

"How is it possible to live," Rilke asks on one occasion, "if the elements of this life are for us completely ungraspable? If we are always inadequate in loving, uncertain in deciding and helpless vis-à-vis death, how is it possible to exist?"[18] Such uncertainty regarding life is not merely verbal. It is expressed in his personal relationships, his homelessness, in the eternal journeys of the ever-restless poet, but also, conversely, in his praise of rootedness, in his many poems on plants—indeed, even in the pathetic attempt at concocting for himself an aristocratic line of descent. His "vie des châteaux" contains both elements: the lack of a permanent residence and dependence on the generosity of others, but also the search for an appropriate haven, his fascination with the nobility, with local history, old houses, furniture, coats of arms, genealogical handbooks and other symbols of rootedness. By refusing to place these extravagances under the rubric of snobbism, his biographer is not merely glossing over the truth: "One of the poet's characteristic traits, and one that might very easily be misunderstood, is seen here in a most revealing light.

Just as there is no question of attributing his predilection for old houses and castles to social prejudice or any similar motive, so we must not suspect his interest in noble families and historic names of having its roots in ordinary, idle snobbishness."[19] Further: "His weakness for the nobility sprang from various impulses—and one can say of him as he himself once said of Proust, whom he admired as few writers of his generation did: 'How narrowly he missed being a snob!'"[20]

The psychological phenomena that accompany this eccentricity are well known. Everyone is aware of the loneliness which the poet, depending on his mood, either sought out or felt condemned to, a loneliness that one cannot choose. One simply is lonely, and the important thing is what one makes out of it.[21] He defined marriage as the uniting of two lonelinesses. And whoever has read the letters written contemporary with the novel knows that Malte's pathological, nervous symptoms, which culminate in the grotesque scene at the Salpêtrière, could not have cost the poet a superhuman effort of the imagination: Rilke himself suffered through them. Indeed, his states of anxiety or exaltation were so persistent that for a time he considered seeking psychoanalytic treatment. In fact, we possess such vivid descriptions of these states that entire books have been constructed around them.[22] We are, in short, thoroughly familiar with the poet's unending dissatisfaction, his neurotic compulsions, his tortuous separation from normal life and his inability to function in that life.

One is therefore astonished to discover that the social scientist characterizes this uprootedness and the complementary desire for rootedness,[23] this anxiety together with a whole series of other symptoms of nervous disturbance, as a widespread mass phenomenon. The will sways back and forth between scruples, inhibitions, and indecisiveness, all of which paralyze action—or it becomes prey to compulsively overdetermined reactions that invest abnormally large amounts of emotional enthusiasm in certain goals and symbols. Such disturbances arise from insecurity and are accompanied by intense states of anxiety and aggression. This language is not taken from the psychological case history of a highly differentiated individual, as one might expect, but rather from the account of a sociologist who is trying to make clear what happens when large numbers of individuals have lost the connection with traditional institutions that is necessary for personal equilibrium and for the smooth functioning of the social apparatus.[24] The resulting social disintegration and lack of relatedness is called *anomie*.[25]

How did it come about that the condition of anomie assumed such dangerously large proportions? It would exceed the limits of this inquiry to elaborate here the entire complex theory of the origins of fascism, but it is nevertheless worthwhile to emphasize some of the central factors with a view to Rilke's possible relation to them. The major cause is seen in the tremendous changes brought about in the lives and activities of huge numbers of people by the industrial revolution. The migration from the country to the rapidly growing cities with their developing slums, the incessant economic crises with their cycles of unemployment, inflation, and war; in the cultural domain, the diminishing influence of the traditionally educated, the spread of mass education and the development of means of mass communication, the dissolution of stable conditions in ethics, religion, and philosophy, the speed with which fashions would change in art, leisure, and consumption—these are only the most obvious phenomena. Constantly threatened by the danger of decline and destruction from the one side, people see on the other a multiplicity of possibilities more oppressive than tempting. Without secure directives for socially sanctioned behavior, many feel attracted to authoritarian movements. Unconditional submission to the authority of a rigid system of belief promises to put an end to the perplexities of life. The escape from freedom that is

PERIOD OF MATURITY

so often discussed is, in no small measure, an escape from anomie.[26]

Rilke's situation, of course, cannot be explained this simply. As an independent artist at the edge of bourgeois society,[27] he was not at the mercy of events to the same degree as someone who pursues a well-defined occupation while settled in a particular country, indeed, in a particular region. But the poet too is only a human being and he is no less cast about by world events than his most unassuming contemporary. Despite his animosity toward the press, Rilke was a quite industrious reader of the news. It was not at all beneath him to now and then send newspaper clippings of a purely political nature to his female correspondents. His carefully cultivated distance vis-à-vis the events of the day—to the degree it was even genuine—did not at all protect him from the convulsions of politics and history. We have already seen what a disturbing effect the war had on him. It would be altogether false to believe that Rilke's interest in external developments ceased when peace came simply because he so loudly proclaimed his withdrawal from the historical arena. An epistolary outburst like the following must be taken entirely seriously.

> The general state of affairs outside in the world [had become] so bad—and, however remote and isolated my old Muzot might seem, I too suffer to the point of sleeplessness from these cruel conflicts, from their hopelessness, and still more from the fact that things are heading again toward "hating," that hate is once again the decisive and effective element in a world which, in order finally to be healed, would require an overflowing of love and tenderness and sheer good will!—The newspapers too have immediately fallen back into the tone of the war years, the paper they are printed on even makes an inflammatory sound when you open it. . . . Where will this lead?[28]

Rilke was a child of his age and his world. Precisely because he attempted to leave behind its historically determined chaos and to attain an eternal order independent of it proves as much. It has been demonstrated that his insecurities reach back to his childhood, and it is likely that they derive from a condition of anomie in his parents' home. Yet, to what degree his choice of an artistic vocation, the mobility that characterized his style of life, his lack of ties to any nation, and the independence of his work which he held to with such determination—to what degree these things are to be evaluated as emancipatory processes I dare not judge.

> Common observation is enough to show that human beings individually and collectively do not react to an "objective" situation in the same way one chemical reacts to another when they are put in a test tube. This form of strict behaviorism is, I submit, just plain wrong. There is always an intervening variable, a filter, one might say, between people and an "objective" situation, made up from all sorts of wants, expectations, and other ideas derived from the past. This intervening variable, which it is convenient to call culture, screens out certain parts of the objective situation and emphasizes other parts.[29]

Nevertheless, it cannot be accidental that Rilke's psychological instability reveals similarities with the mass phenomena described by sociologists. As a sensitive artist, as an unbourgeois, visionary poet, as a driven *poète maudit*, he was *per definitionem* a modern individual living in a state of anomie. In addition, because of his intellectual talent and his nervous organization, he was exposed to every influence and sensed within himself every problem of his age. For these reasons he acquires a symptomatic significance for his epoch. As Ulrich Fülleborn has stated, ". . . there is hardly an intellectual problem of the beginning twentieth century which does not reappear as a theme in Rilke's work and find there a solution."[30]

Under the umbrella term "modernity" we include such

PERIOD OF MATURITY 53

features as large cities, technology, and certain social and economic phenomena that have given modern life its unmistakable character. In the foregoing section we attempted to relate Rilke's rootlessness and perplexity to a specific mass phenomenon, so-called anomie. To be sure, in so doing we have placed his lack of direction within a larger context, but we have not yet made plausible those fascist inclinations that he expressed in the final years of his life.

In the course of our investigation we saw how, for a brief period at war's end in Munich, Rilke even flirted with the Leftists; we likewise saw what factors prevented him from further *engagement*. One must keep in mind that in the case of a political outsider whose participation in events is emotional and verbal, the borders between political ideologies are not as clearly drawn as for a contemporary who fully involves himself to the point of being prepared to take action. Even in the case of the latter, the line of demarcation between "left" and "right" is not always precise. Otherwise it would not be such a common observation that the independent intelligentsia on both sides revealed more similarities than they themselves were willing to acknowledge—perhaps one ought to say than they *could*, in the heat of encounter, take cognizance of.

> Comparison reveals that the independent intelligentsia of left and right had more in common than they cared to admit. Both groups came to socialism *malgré eux*, not because of clearly formulated class interest but because of their strong humanistic convictions. The ethical impossibility of capitalism motivated both. Both espoused revolution out of frustration—frustration not with class rule but with liberal democratic institutions that did not work. The left encouraged social revolution to realize the traditional bourgeois aims of political democracy, the right urged a political revolution to realize the traditional bourgeois aims of social community.[31]

Rilke's historical position, then, needs to be characterized more precisely.

We must first of all indicate—even if only in terms of a few key notions—what was behind these phenomena. It is important to realize that anomie is not produced by forces that just happen to become efficacious in the life of society, but rather that it is the by-product of a process characteristic for the West in general, a process that social theorists call rationalization.[32] This new element emerges fully in the natural sciences; from there it exerts a revolutionary influence on traditional views regarding the nature of the world. It assumes especially wide resonance in its application to technology. Money becomes a central value and, in the final analysis, the newly achieved mobility of all goods serves a single end: the acquisition of property. This goes so far that art also becomes a commodity. In general, the influence of these developments on culture is not to be underestimated. Philosophical and religious belief systems that had remained valid for centuries are shaken. A general tendency toward the elimination of symbolic relations asserts itself.

A further source of anomie is the ideology of the Leftists, which increasingly pledges itself to the rationalization of life in order to dismantle inherited ideas. The main targets attacked with the aid of this arsenal of new ideas are the bastions of traditional privileges: authority and caste prerogatives. A forceful and effective emancipatory movement begins to liberate the individual from all powers that do not have the sanction of reason. Science becomes the prototype of every rational form of knowledge, while all those elements of tradition that cannot be scientifically grounded are submitted to an aggressive denunciation, demythologization, devaluation.

In the earliest phases of this development, the rationalistic mode of thought is primarily associated with positive values. Visions of a splendid social order of the future develop: a future where freedom will triumph over tyranny, enlightenment over ignorance and superstition, equality and justice over privilege, and a free economy over monopolies and all the irrational limitations set on trade and enterprise by custom and tradition.

Gradually, however, a pronounced shift begins to take place, mainly on account of changes within the rationalized economic organization itself. Instead of magically producing universal happiness, the emancipation of the economy from monopoly and tradition led in fact to a system of capitalist exploitation, to new forms of domination and unjust privilege. Liberation from the House of Bourbon brought forth a new enslavement perpetrated by the executive committees of the bourgeoisie. The critics of this new development declared capitalism to be the cause of every social ill, thereby elevating it to an all-encompassing symbol comparable to original sin. "Profit" became the key word that explained every evil. "Left" became the equivalent of "positivistic" and "utilitarian."

Above all, it became apparent that rationalism was not sufficient to formulate all the values important to our society. It neglected the so-called nonlogical aspects of human conduct: the emotional life, the traditions of the family, the customs of intimate social behavior, the nuances of social hierarchy, regional, ethnic and national peculiarities, and especially religion.

It was on this level, then, that a strong reactionary tendency developed. The neglect of traditional values had gone further than many members of society could accept. Capitalism was seen as the logical consequence and not as a perversion of the rationalization process, and in this way both capitalism and its leftist opponent could be treated as secret brothers and as common enemies. The Jews, who play a major role in both systems, embodied the union of the two in the mind of the reactionaries.

Reactionary opposition to the rationalization of social processes and relations is one of the main features of the fascist movements. In its essential points such opposition accepts the socialist condemnation of the dominant order, but includes as part of this rejected order not only capitalism but also left radicalism and the entire climate of scientific and philosophical rationalism. (The radical left, on the other hand, views capitalism and fascism as a unity.)[33]

These are in general outline the fundamental propositions of the noncommunist theory of fascism. Beyond these findings there is, of course, a good deal of talk about social classes, economic factors, and the greater or lesser susceptibility of certain vocational or social groups to fascism. Sauer, who supports the thesis that the fascists are the losers of the industrial revolution, summarizes his views in a form with which, as far as I can tell, most researchers in the field would agree: "Fascist movements represented the reaction of the lower-class losers, while the upper-class losers tended to react in a non-fascist way, but were potential allies of fascist regimes."[34] For Rilke—and therefore for our investigation here—this distinction is probably not of fundamental importance. He came from a mixed milieu, closer to the first group but complicated by the German-Slavic opposition. In later life, however, he moved mainly among the second group to which his patrons and friends belonged. His vacillating inclinations might have to do with the conflicts between these two classes but they can also be explained by his life as an independent writer detached from any binding class allegiance.[35]

We can best grasp the problem by adhering to concrete questions. In this regard, another of Sauer's findings is especially revealing for our inquiry: "As a movement of losers, it turned against technological progress and economic growth; it tried to stop or even to reverse the trend toward industrialization and to return to the earlier, 'natural' ways of life."[36] Many scholars in the field single out attacks on the culture of the large cities and on technology, coupled with racist and nationalistic interpretations of reality as cen-

PERIOD OF MATURITY 57

tral points in the rightist ideology. Another much investigated factor which is of importance for our inquiry is the ambivalent relationship of the rightest movements to the problems of social hierarchy and social revolution. Sauer speaks of the "intriguing paradox of a revolutionary mass movement whose goals were antirevolutionary in the classical sense."[37] Here we have a point of departure from which we can proceed to compare Rilke's attitude toward each of the relevant factors.[38]

The City

Every reader of Rilke's works is familiar with the poet's abhorrence of the large city. He only held out in Paris for so many years through self-discipline, as it were, in a kind of self-imposed trial. He was moved by a stoic will to endure to the end the task imposed on him precisely because it was so terrible. Like many before and after him, he succumbed then to the magic of the "Ville lumière" and even after the war returned there twice, full of nostalgia. But these are biographical matters. Rilke's ideology was unequivocally opposed to the large modern city. In this regard one need only recall *Malte* and the *Book of Hours*, both of which came into being under the impact of the poet's first Paris experience. The city appears as the terrifying scenery of life in the modern industrial world, of a reality stripped of every magic: a place full of hospitals, old-age homes, mortuaries and every sort of ugliness, the playground of all the disinherited and fallen, of cripples and other dehumanized, disease-ridden creatures. The castles, on the other hand, became the symbolic sites of the old, healthy, prerevolutionary world. Malte, the typical *déclassé*, lives between these two worlds and has a difficult time doing so. His aristocratic world has dissolved and in Paris he is in constant danger of being swept into the dustbin of modern life, of being counted among the "throwaways,"[39] who secretly and much to his horror already regard him as one of their own despite the fact that his collar is fresh and his hand, became the symbolic sites of the old, healthy, prerevolutionary world. Malte, the typical *déclassé*, lives belook at me and know it,"[40] he remarks in astonishment. But they are right, for his "old furniture rots in a barn, . . . and I too, yes, my God, I have no roof over me and it rains into my eyes."[41] This same danger of demise and proletarization, which we find represented here so graphically, was the horror of many who had once had it better and who sought to escape from their lower status into fascism.

But whoever wants to learn in detail how the cities were fashioned and what they made of the people condemned to spend their miserable bit of existence there should turn to the grandiloquent invectives of the book "Of Poverty and Of Death" from the *Book of Hours*.[42] There we hear of the "anxiety of the cities" and of "their meager time," which is exactly the opposite of the "grand time" that Rilke searched for throughout his life.[43] "There the people live in misery and burdened" and "children . . . don't know that outside flowers call."[44] "The large cities are not true,"[45] everything about them is an illusion: the day in the cities is not the real day, the night is not the night, the rich people are not rich and the poor are not truly poor. And in the cities everything can be bought. "The cities . . . use up burning many peoples."

> And their people serve in cultures
> and fall deeply from balance and measure
> and call their snail's traces progress
> and drive faster, where they once drove slowly,
> and they have feelings and sparkle like whores
> and make still louder noise with metal and with glass.[46]

In short, "the large cities are cities lost and dissolved."[47] There is little purpose in quoting further passages and removing from context statements that are much more effective when viewed within the whole work. We merely want to cast a brief glance at the nonmetropolitan world which also appears in these poems. It is the world

> . . . of the shepherd peoples,
> the ones who beclouded the clear, green plains
> when with their dusky bustle of sheep
> they moved across them like a morning sky.
> And when they camped and the commands
> had fallen silent in the new night,
> it was as if another soul
> had awakened in their flat land of wandering—:
> the high dark trains of camels
> surrounded it in the mountain splendor.[48]

It is a natural, patriarchal, Biblical world, close to the earth, to the animals, the plants, and to God. In this way Rilke makes use of an age-old literary tradition to express his own despair before the forms of modern life: the topos, which in the Bible juxtaposes the solitude of the desert with sinful Babylon, which in the idylls of antiquity contrasts the pastoral life with the metropolis, and which the Christian moralists reworked as the opposition between village and court,[49] becomes in its late capitalist form the contrast of country and city.

Technology

Rilke's abhorrence of machines, of everything that has to do with technology and mechanics, is no less well known than his dread of the city. The references to metal, glass, fast driving and progress in the above quoted passage from the *Book of Hours* can be taken as representative for countless others that express similar feelings. A famous formulation of his irreconcilable resistance to technological advance occurs in the long letter of self-interpretation he wrote to the Polish translator of the *Elegies*, Witold von

Hulewics. There he describes things from America, the technical country *par excellence*, as "appearance-things, life-dummies." Indeed, he even goes so far as to deny the American apple its authenticity.[50]

The British critic, Eudo C. Mason, has ascertained that Rilke disliked the entire Anglo-Saxon world because he suspected it of being more complicitous than any other with the modern technical mechanization of life. "American," this critic suggests, was

> Rilke's favourite word for those tendencies in modern civilization which he was most afraid of and repelled by.... It is directed not so much against the people themselves as against the mechanizing processes which have originated amongst them, and which they find themselves compelled to accept and serve.... In this sense, Rilke sees 'Americanism' all around him on the European continent, too, dominating more and more influential groups of the continental peoples, and destined in the end to subdue them all.[51]

Where Rilke does praise the machine, he does so only because he had arrived at a position of seeing "... the supreme mission of the poet to praise *everything*, without discrimination, that is to say, above all, to praise what is most terrifying, suspect and odious to him, ..."[52] just as in a poem to Baudelaire he admires the poet for "celebrating even that which hurts him."[53] Indeed, in the *Sonnets to Orpheus*, Rilke not only praises the machine, but also cruelty, disgusting diseases, betrayal, begging, the death penalty, the decomposition of corpses, and many other ghastly things. "It is almost conceivable," our British critic adds with angry wit, "that at such a moment he might even have brought himself to bestow his blessing upon the English language." We shall again encounter this phenomenon which Rilke dubbed "completeness" and which helped him tolerate the most awful social ills. Here let us simply note that his attitude, translated into political terms, corresponds to an unyielding conservatism, a clinging to the *status quo* at any price.

Rilke's aversion to mechanization was shared by millions from the preindustrial branches of employment and by their ideologues. Like Rilke, they tended toward an ever more despairing radical and aggressive conservatism which often enough led them into the various national fascist movements.

What Rilke feared, of course, was not merely the disappearance of beautiful, handmade things. He felt that the machine made it ever more difficult, and finally impossible, for the sensitive soul to find its way in an external world now completely destroyed. Beyond this, he was conscious of far-reaching changes in the social structure that derived from the same basic forces and that were bound to transform the function and nature of art. He saw himself before "a public upon which so much incomplete and false and calculated artistic production has been dumped and which does not have the time nor the aptitude to be more attentive and receptive to something authentic, wherever it might make its way through to them in this throng, than to something conspicuous perhaps or something that is seductive with lesser means."[54] He foresaw the demise of the elitist poet who, supported by a noble patron, produces profound and hermetic works for a tiny minority of highly educated individuals. He saw a time approaching when the highest value that he knew, the inner development of the individual, would count for nothing—a time when "everything would aim at the expropriation of individual abilities, whereby of course all that we now call art and mind would appear eliminated, along with all the inner spaces of emotion and of heartfelt decor."[55]

In another letter Rilke associates art and religion exactly in the sense we refer to here:

> Yesterday Eisner had called together a meeting. . . , the hall proved to be too small and so people gathered beneath the night sky, nearly seven thousand of them. . . . Now each of us certainly stands with those who want the most honest and the most thoroughgoing changes, but I doubt whether they can still be brought about peacefully at this late date and against such obstinate resistance; if they come about violently, then a new destruction will be added to all the others, one which would shatter things we value highly. Art is always the one who promises the most distant future, or at least a future beyond the next one, and for that reason a crowd that passionately seizes after what is most immediate will always be iconoclastic. To the untrained and eager view the power of that which is entirely of the future looks so much like the authority of the past that the two are bound to be confused. . . .[56]

Heine had already expressed himself similarly on the subject of revolutions. Rilke speaks here as an educated bourgeois who turns to the Social Democrats because, on the one hand, he recognizes the necessity of social reforms and, on the other, he fears radical revolutions for the sake of art and mind. Such statements, of course, belong to Rilke's "World War Period." It is not at all surprising, then, that Rilke sought to impede this overall development in the nature and function of art, nor that in his search he turned to those forces from which he could expect aid—according to his own experience and education—for the values of poetry and soulfulness. That he was not alone in this effort, that many poets succumbed to the same error—above all the great lyric poets of his epoch—is common knowledge. Hofmannsthal and George, Mallarmé and Valéry, Yeats, Pound and Eliot[57]—all of them were, either from early on or in the end, in the archconservative camp, some of them even in fascist parties.

Rilke's nightmarish vision of "machines suppressing our hands"[58] may well be the same one that troubled the Imperial Union of German Handworkers, but we must not forget that for Rilke it was primarily a question of his own handwork, a handwork done in words.

Social Aspects

One of Rilke's biographers remarks that a "peasant girl, a maidservant" meant as much to the poet "as a princess," that to him "a working man was as important as an artist." To be sure, he follows this up with a stipulation: they were all equal in Rilke's eyes "provided that each was genuinely and entirely peasant girl, maidservant, princess, worker or artist."[59] If that means anything at all, then it is probably this: the various social classes exhibit definite traits; every individual must be imprinted with this configuration of class traits and must under no circumstances endeavor to move beyond his class-determined sphere. Surprisingly enough, Rilke himself confirms this interpretation. We have already encountered his peculiar notion of poverty and human misery in relatively early works such as *Two Stories of Prague*, the *Stories of Our Dear Lord*, in the *Book of Hours*, and in *Malte*.

Two years before his death, the poet once again summarized these ideas in a general statement, so detailed that it constitutes something like a social theory, which in any case affords insight into his rigid and, at the same time, utterly naïve conception of social issues. In 1924 a young German scholar initiated a correspondence with Rilke and succeeded in convincing the poet to reply to a sort of questionnaire.[60] One question was posed as follows: "What influenced the strong social interests that come to expression in *Wegwarten*?"[61] Rilke was so unpleasantly affected by the implications of the word "social" that he spent an entire treatise defending himself against them. He asserts:

> ... that it would be incorrect to classify any of my endeavors under this rubric. To be sure, an element of human congeniality, a brotherly element, is involuntary for me and must be a predisposition of my nature.... However, what thoroughly distinguishes such a joyful and natural devotion from the social, as people understand it, is the *complete lack of desire, indeed the disinclination, to change or, as it is expressed, to improve anyone's situation.*[62] No one's situation in the world is such that it could not prove uniquely useful to his soul.[63] It seems to me it will create nothing but disorder if the general effort (an illusion besides!) should presume to lighten or to eliminate schematically men's afflictions, an undertaking which more severely encroaches upon the freedom of the other than the state of want itself does, which, with indescribable accommodations and almost tenderly, gives to whomever entrusts himself to it directives as to how it might be escaped from—if not outwardly, then inwardly.... To claim to change, to improve the situation of a human being, means to offer him in exchange for difficulties in which he is experienced and practiced other difficulties which perhaps will find him more helpless still.[64] If I have sometimes been able to express the imaginary voices of the dwarf or beggar in the form of my own emotion,[65] then the metal for this casting-into-form was not taken from the wish that the dwarf or the beggar might have things less burdensome; on the contrary, only by praising their incomparable destinies could the poet who had suddenly identified with them be true and thorough, and there was nothing he had to fear and reject more than a corrected world in which the dwarfs are stretched and the beggars enriched. The god of completeness will see to it that these varieties[66] do not cease to exist, and it would be the most superficial way of looking at the matter to consider the poet's joy at this suffering abundance an aesthetic excuse. Thus my conscience is clear before every accusation of escapism when I wholly claim for my poem, as regards the concepts "rich" and "poor," the legitimate impartiality of

artistic expression. It could never have been my intention to play off the poor against the rich, or to make my avowal of greater conviction on behalf of the one than the other. It may well have been given to me, however, to measure poverty and wealth for a while according to their purest standards,[67] for how could it, here as well, turn out otherwise than that both be praised if both are genuinely known.

In a world that attempts to dissolve the divine into a sort of anonymity, that humanitarian overestimation, which expects of human aid what it cannot give, had to gain ground. And divine kindness is so indescribably bound up with divine harshness that an age that—preempting providence[68]—undertakes to distribute the former simultaneously drags the most ancient stores of cruelty among mankind. (We've experienced this.)[69]

A political scientist could find copious material here for analysis. What Rilke is aiming at is a rejection of every form of social change, indeed even of the mildest palliative of the welfare state. This reply to an innocent questionnaire is an unconditional affirmation of the social *status quo*.

Rilke's concept of the beggar echoes the high estimation of this figure in medieval times—a phenomenon we also encounter in certain modern writers such as Adalbert Stifter—in that poverty is willed by God. However, Rilke's position differs from the Christian one by virtue of its radical, individualistic solipsism. The charitable alleviation of misery is no longer the means that the *others*—those who have things better—make use of in order to reach heaven, but instead is only an end in itself for the person burdened by misery, an activity that provides him with some sort of soulful stimulus.

Rilke is to be distinguished from the social-Darwinist proponents of *laissez-faire* who regard poverty as a just consequence of—practically as a punishment for—greater stupidity or lesser ability. His formula is ideal for all those who, for whatever reasons, want to withdraw themselves from social responsibility without giving up the spectacle of the tragedies that are played out within society. Poverty is a phenomenon that has nothing to do with the social world, a phenomenon for which it makes no sense to search out causes and try to do away with them. With this statement written in later life, the theodicy introduced in the poet's youth achieves its completion: poverty is a combination of religious and aesthetic elements. The god of completeness decrees that everything should be in order that the world be beautiful and bountiful, but also in order that those who are immediately affected might have an opportunity to achieve for themselves a kind of paradise by exploiting the deformations with which they are afflicted for the greater refinement and subtlety of their souls. The source of all human defects is nothing less than nature itself. For that reason dwarfs and beggars are put in a *single* pot. We shouldn't want to enrich the latter any more than we can stretch the former. Rilke's confidence in any intervention in the mechanisms of society is so limited because he conceives of society as an *organism*. From the *Stories of Our Dear Lord* on, poverty is viewed as a private matter with which one cannot tamper without the risk of bringing about more ill than good. Whoever manipulates society—apparently he assumes this doesn't normally happen—ends up where the Russian Revolution did.[70]

Rilke sees the aesthetic component of this doctrine in the "impartiality" of poverty and wealth, which he is justified in claiming for himself "with a clear conscience." Here, however, the ethical and the aesthetic standpoints are not in opposition, as Rilke believes. It is not that moral sympathy is overcome for the sake of an artistic sympathy; rather, the imagination itself, that is to say, the poetic, simply fails. Rilke's fear of specific changes and developments within society quite apparently dulled his own perception of the *disadvantages* of poverty and influenced his aesthetic credo. Just as "apolitical" behavior becomes of necessity "political" in this turbulent age, so too "impartiality" vis-à-vis rich and poor is in fact partiality for the rich. Having arrived at this central point of our investigation, we can already conclude, even at this early stage of our inquiry, that there exists a relationship between poetic "praise" on the one hand and a definable socio-political position on the other.

Fortunately Rilke sometimes departed in practice from the inhumane principle—even if it is such only out of blindness—that one should not help other human beings. These departures corresponded entirely to his own definition of the concept "social." Once, he took up the cause of a peace movement which he held in great esteem:

> I saw Annette [Kolb] day before yesterday and she spoke to me about a "project".... She is determined to engage herself actively in this undertaking and *such a cause concerns all of us without question*. In the course of a recent meeting held in Munich some intellectuals and various other persons animated by the same spirit decided to establish an international review; Romain Rolland, Shaw, van Eeden and several other foreign "enemies" have been notified and they have promised their assistance.... I said to myself that you could win a few of your friends for this cause.[71]

On another occasion he even sought the advice of a politician decried as leftist on how best to help people who have been severely disadvantaged without rubbing in the unpleasantness of their situation. In this case his worldliness and sense of tact proved their efficacy; he was not yet entirely ossified by his dogmatic inwardness. His friend and hostess Hertha König had conceived a plan to establish a charitable institution to aid the many outcasts created by the war. However, it was questionable whether Count Baudissin zu Stolp in Pomerania could be asked to serve as the founder of this so-called "domestic army." Certain problems related to this plan immediately came to mind: a welfare institution called into being by aristocratic landowners and directed by government employees would hardly correspond to Hertha König's original conception of an institution close to the people. Rilke's letter was addressed to Kurt Eisner—the leader of the Munich Council Republic who was later murdered. In it Rilke suggested that the responsibility for the charitable enterprise be given to the representatives of the disadvantaged themselves in order to ensure optimal trust and a just distribution of the aid.[72] Both of these "social" actions, however, took place during the war years, the period of Rilke's life during which he was most alert to matters of social concern.[73] But later on he reverted to the most unyielding conception of the social.

From all of this it must be concluded that Rilke did not advocate revolutionary intervention in the course of world history. A quick glance at his more or less unequivocal condemnation of the Russian Revolution confirms this point from another angle. Most of his statements regarding the Revolution are passing remarks woven into letters whose recipients he could probably count on to hold similar opinions. Examples are the "We've experienced this" quoted above, or the lapidary "The Soviets have shown us where the path of liberty leads" of the *Lettres Milanaises*,[74] or his remark to an *émigré* comparing the Russian Revolution to the "Tatarschina," the yoke of the Tartars from which "the authentic, the ever-surviving Russia" will gradually extricate itself.[75] Only once does he seem to express himself positively on the Revolution. This occurs in his correspondence with a Herr von W., who had apparently arranged to have Blok's poem "The Scythians" sent to Rilke. Rilke acknowledges receipt of the "magnificent poem," calling it testimony to a fact

> ... that I have hoped during all these terrible years might in this way and in no other come to pass on that Russian ground that is so thoroughly sanctified for me; Russia, in

PERIOD OF MATURITY 69

accordance with her deeper task and gifts, has been the only nation to have taken upon herself the entire, infinite suffering and to have transformed herself in doing so. *What* the result of her surviving on the basis of this suffering will be cannot be foreseen, but it will be altogether different from this Western sneaking-by. —Indeed, now it has become wretchedly clear how intellectual lack of principle has increasingly become for the West its refuge, its flight from the realities of the suffering we are condemned to and of the earnest, finite joy. . . . Well, you know all that, you even say it. . . .[76]

Since the political poem "The Scythians" by Aleksandr Aleksandrovič Blok warns the West against military action aimed at revolutionary Russia, this passage must count as Rilke's friendliest statement concerning the new Soviet nation. We do not know what considerations regarding Herr von W. motivated Rilke; it is certain, though, that these formulations bespeak a most ephemeral good will. Rilke's early dislike of external interventions in the social and economic circumstances of the individual underwent a slight corrective adjustment only during the war years. In his most mature period he intensified the conservatism to which he had long since been predisposed to an inflexibility exceeding everything that had gone before.

There is, however, another intimate document available to us in which the problem is raised from within, that is, from the perspective of the disadvantaged individual himself. The young laborer who, like Hofmannsthal's Chandos, writes this fictive letter,[77] is a most unexpected mask for Rilke which allows him to set forth his own concerns. Most of the reflections contained in the letter have to do with religious questions. In accord with Rilke's emphatic individualism, the historical Christ is declared incompetent to grasp the special exigencies of the twentieth century and is rejected as a mediator between the individual human being and God. This letter is unsurpassed in importance as a document of Rilke's personal coming-to-terms with Christianity. The letter also contains highly interesting reflections on temporal power. There is only *one* means to counter it, this unlikely factory worker declares, namely "to go further than it does." And then follows the detailed explication of this cryptic thesis:

> One should endeavor to see in every power that claims a right over us all power, the entire power, the power of God. One should say to oneself: there is only *one*, and one should understand the limited, the false, the mistaken power as if it were that which justifiably seizes hold of us. In this way wouldn't it become harmless? If one always sees in every power, even in wicked and mean power, if one sees power itself, I mean that which in the end proves to have the right to be powerful, wouldn't one survive then, unblemished so to speak, even the unjust and the despotic?

In order to assuage the reader's growing scepticism, the writer interjects a concession: "I'm young and there's much rebellion within me; I cannot assure you that I act according to my insight in every case where impatience and dissatisfaction sweep me along." But these are reprehensible passions. His principles alone are correct:

> ... I know that submission leads further than rebellion; it shames, which is a way of taking possession of power, and it contributes indescribably to the glorification of the just power. The rebel forces himself outside the range of attraction of a power center, and perhaps he succeeds in leaving this force field altogether; but afterwards he stands in emptiness and has to look about for other gravitations that might draw him into a relationship. And these are usually of lesser inner lawfulness than the first. Why not then see right away, in the one in which we find ourselves, the greatest power, and not be disconcerted by its weaknesses and waverings? At some point despotism comes up against the law on its own, and we save energy if we leave it up to despotism to bring about its own conversion.[78]

PERIOD OF MATURITY

Any commentary here would be superfluous. This is divine forgiveness for every earthly abuse, the renunciation of temporal justice and law, the legitimation of every order merely for the sake of order, acquiescence in advance to every sort of human enslavement whatever means it might employ.

This effort from the year 1922, together with the above quoted reply to the questionnaire regarding the "social," and the letters on Mussolini from the year of his death represent Rilke's political last will and testament. It is the modern version of a strict Lutheranism:[79] on the basis of religious convictions regarding the relationship between law and authority, every imaginable concession is made to worldly power, even the most corrupt. In addition, despite the most severe suffering caused by the perversity of external circumstances, every wish for liberation, no matter how hesitating, is resolutely relegated to an invisible internal realm.

In previous sections we have continued to ask how Rilke's specific inclinations are related to fascism. If, in view of this extremely quietistic notion of social order, we again raise this question, we recognize not only that Rilke's notion provided no obstacle whatsoever to fascism, but also that it exactly expresses the state of consciousness required to push the adherents of a "conservative revolution" over the line to fascism. One historian has offered the following assessment of such circles in Germany:

> [They] did not come from the lower classes of the population. On the contrary, they were men and women who wanted to maintain their property and their superior status over the working classes. The notion of a genuine social revolution was anathema to these people, yet they were profoundly dissatisfied with their world. The tension between their desire to preserve their status and their equally fervent desire to alter society was resolved by the appeal to a spiritual revolution which would revitalize the nation without revolutionizing its structure.[80]

We need only remove from this analysis those roughly cut aspects tailored to the description of broad population groups in order to recognize its astonishing applicability to Rilke's world-view.

The Jews

Antipathy toward the people of the Bible runs through all of occidental history. Throughout the course of changing economic and cultural systems only the form of this antipathy has changed; the phenomenon itself has remained constant. This prejudice has had such a pervasive effect upon the western peoples that no geographical region, no class nor caste has remained untouched by it, absurdly enough not even its victims, the Jews themselves. Although anti-Semitism is distributed across the entire political spectrum, it quite evidently increases in significance, complexity, and intensity as we move from left to right. After all, the Jewish emancipation was always tied to the rationalist, leftist movements (to mention just this one, quite obvious reason). According to its manner and degree of virulence, therefore, anti-Semitism can serve very well as an instrument for exposing otherwise hidden political passions.

Anti-Semitism played an important role in almost all varieties of fascism, in some even the central role, uniting victoriously beneath its banner all the separate and disputing rightist factions.[81] This was not the case, however, in early Italian fascism, and it should be emphasized that in the course of his long-winded apology for Mussolini's regime Rilke finds time to put in a good word for the Jews.[82]

Nevertheless, I have to classify Rilke among the moderate anti-Semites. Here, once again, that sensitive needle of Rilke's "recording instrument" does not hold to one position but vibrates back and forth. As early as the *Stories of Our Dear Lord* we had an opportunity to view the Jews according to Rilke's divided perspective: as parasites on the body of the Ukrainian people or in the figure of the honorable religious seer Melchisedech, depending on whether one holds before one the "Song of Justice" or "A Scene from the Venice Ghetto." But these were the youthful efforts of an immature spirit. If instead we focus on Rilke's encounter with the Jewish poet Franz Werfel and its reflection in his correspondence, then the year is 1913 and we are dealing with a mature Rilke of thirty-eight. It is not a matter here of assessing the literary-historical significance of this encounter, which has already been dealt with elsewhere.[83] As far as literary matters are concerned, we merely want to keep in mind that Rilke was enthusiastic about Werfel's poems and that he saw in his Prague compatriot the only poet of the expressionist generation from whom he could hope for a continuation of his own poetic endeavors. His ensuing disappointment is usually attributed by critics to Werfel's humanism, which was opposed to Rilke's antihumanistic stance. Regarding Rilke's anti-Semitic reaction to Werfel, however, silence reigns. And yet this too played a role. It is as if a battle were taking place within Rilke between his high esteem for the *poet* Werfel and his aversion to Werfel the *Jew*. He was himself half conscious of the injustice he committed; otherwise he would not have written to the Princess Thurn und Taxis as follows: "But the value of his *oeuvre* is such that it will doubtless be possible for me one day or another to reestablish a less rancorous and more valid point of view toward him than the one I occupy at present."[84] And in fact three months later, as predicted, he can offer high praise for Werfel's work and at the same time report of the person that "everything else [is] only the accidental young human being which he is working himself out of."[85]

As a young literary busybody in Prague, Rilke himself cannot have been a tremendously likable figure and, indeed, his conduct at that time has been sufficiently criticized. Never, though, did it occur to anyone to hold characteristics of his race or blood responsible for that episode. But this is precisely what Rilke does in the case of Werfel; how he does it is what is truly alarming.[86] In his long letter of October 21, 1913 to the Princess he begins with a factual account of how he had repeatedly seen Werfel in Hellerau and Dresden. Then in the next sentence he switches to the central theme: the Baroness Nadherny, who was also there, had called Werfel a "Judenbub" (a Jewish scamp—the word appears in German in the letter, which is otherwise composed in French) and the sad thing about that was, Rilke opines, that she was not altogether wrong. He, Rilke, had been on the verge of opening his arms to the youth, but instead he folded them behind his back, like an indifferent person taking a walk. Ten times a day he reminded himself that it had been Werfel who had accomplished so many poetic miracles. In his absence, it was even possible for Rilke to muster enthusiasm for Werfel, but once he was actually present Rilke felt so embarrassed that he could not even look him in the eye. For the sake of precision, we must quote directly the turns of phrase Rilke employs to justify this peculiar feeling:

> However he was not at all dislikable, extremely intelligent, too intelligent perhaps for his poetry, which, if it has been considered too finely, too deviously calculated, has suffered on account of a Jewish spirit which is all too familiar with merchandise. . . . I felt for the first time the duplicity of the Jewish mentality, which feels detached from everything that holds us and which manages to speak about those things nevertheless; nourished by a quasi-negative experience, this spirit which penetrates things and nevertheless does not truly possess them, like the poison which enters everywhere taking revenge for not being part of the organism.[87]

Here we run up against an entire series of the most popular anti-Semitic clichés: there is something almost physically repulsive about the Jews; suspecting nothing and

PERIOD OF MATURITY

well-intentioned, you meet up with one and, although there is nothing dislikable about the fellow in any usual sense, you nevertheless recoil in disgust from the aura he emits. The Jew is highly intelligent, this much is acknowledged, but too intelligent for poetry! Here, a number of ideas resonate between the lines: poetry, genuine poetry, is something intuitive and unreflective that emerges from the depths of the soul—"dictation" is what Rilke will later call it. But the Jew is and remains a rationalist. Should the two—that is, Judaism and poetry—converge, then the result is mere manufacture. The Jew behaves *as if* he were an inspired creator who brings forth his products out of irrational depths, but that is only skillful pretense carried on for business purposes. For the Jew regards poems—as he does everything else as well—from the standpoint of business. To make a commodity of poetry is certainly a crime in the eyes of someone who could say of himself: "Just the awareness that there exists a relationship between my writing and the day's necessities is enough to make working impossible for me." To be sure, this statement of Rilke's itself awakens socio-historical echoes in which the trained ear hears the expression of a specific attitude that was by no means limited to a single individual.[88] The central point is, however, that it was only due to Werfel's Jewishness that the equation of poetry and merchandise crossed Rilke's mind at all! Nevertheless, Rilke then embarks upon a meandering interpretation that hardly differs from the most perfidious insinuations of the Nazis. He speaks of the mendacity and the rootless negativism of the Jewish spirit, which never authentically participates in anything but always has something to say; of Jewish parasitism that, to get revenge for its exclusion from the organism, exerts its poisonous effects everywhere.

These invectives are an isolated instance as far as their amplitude is concerned, but not in their basic thrust. Cynical anti-Semitic slurs against the poet Ernst Lissauer, a long letter warning the Baroness Sidonie Nadherny not to marry Karl Kraus who is separated from her by "an ultimate, ineradicable difference," whining about the "nouveaux riches, Jews mostly,"[89] who ruin his stay at the once so exclusive resort of Ragaz—these indices testify to an antipathy that was constantly on the verge of breaking out, that was in all likelihood instigated in his childhood,[90] and that continued to grow into the last years of his life. As late as 1924 it expresses itself in an especially grotesque manner. The theme is psychoanalysis, "where the *How* is of indescribable importance." Then follows the complaint: "What all isn't being done, especially in its Jewish version, in the name of psychoanalysis." "Frau Andreas," Rilke emphasizes, in order to show how miserable the situation is, is "the only non-Jew who practices these treatments. . . ."[91] How absurd this is when one considers the origins of this therapy. The Nazis were only more thorough with their wholesale condemnation of Freudianism: person, theory, and practice. The letter containing this statement is once again addressed to the Princess Marie Thurn und Taxis, which lends support to the view of Ilse Blumenthal-Weiss (herself the recipient of two long Rilkean epistles on Judaism) that Rilke was accommodating himself to the expectations of the Princess, "who approved of the usual social anti-Semitism of the aristocracy."[92]

Do such examples of monstrousness become any more acceptable if we assume that Rilke invented them to please his royal correspondent? We will do well to withhold all speculation here and adhere to the facts. The fact is that Rilke often adapted himself to his correspondents and sometimes wrote what they wanted to hear. In his youth this practice sometimes produced rather ugly contradictions. For instance, in April, 1896, he writes: "It is very important to me to hear the judgment of the author of *Liebelei* whom I esteem so highly." In June of the same year he refers to this same poet as a "literary parvenu," adding:

PERIOD OF MATURITY

"In one or two years, if things turn out halfway just, Arthur Schnitzler will be humbly waiting in the antechamber of the dramaturge Jenny. . . ."[93] Is it necessary to say who the recipients of the two letters were? This exceeds in "duplicity" anything the young Werfel might have done or said. But with increasing age, such slips become less frequent and finally disappear entirely, giving way to an uncomplicated and in part heartfelt participation in the concerns and needs of his correspondents. It is true that in his last years Rilke quite obviously composed his letters with a view to their eventual publication and that he explicitly released them for this purpose in his will. However, who among us could look forward with certainty to the publication of his or her entire correspondence knowing that he or she would fare any better than Rilke?

For the sake of balance, let us turn now to a more discriminating correspondence in which Rilke allegedly did full justice to the Jews. In fact, his two long epistles on Judaism do contain some positive points. The thoughts expressed there can be subdivided into three groups: religious, historical, and racial. The basic religious conception is an idea that Rilke was very fond of, which recurs again and again in his writings:[94] there are peoples among whom religion and nationality constitute an "innate unity," peoples "who did *not* come to God through belief, but rather experienced God by means of their own national identity."[95] Among these "favored" peoples are those of the Near East and of ancient Mexico, to a certain degree the orthodox Russians, the Scandinavians, the Spaniards, the Arabs, and also the Jews. He possesses "an indescribable trust" in such proples; he "envies" them. To be sure, this felicitous unity has long since been lost (though it is never said why) and the Jews have become entirely different. The exposition that follows is especially noteworthy as it is among those rare instances where Rilke regards the nature of man not as something fixed but as something that is shaped, at least in part, by historical influences, that is, as a reaction to concrete, unavoidable social factors. This historical dimension of Rilke's explanation of the Jewish nature and destiny is, however, fused in a most curious way with the commonplaces of anti-Semitic racist doctrine. The result is a passage of incredible iridescence, extremely ambiguous as regards the values it affirms. An immensely talented master of syntax is at work, a stylist who, with the precision of a pharmacist, here adds and there removes a tiny grain so that the scale always holds a precarious balance and one is uncertain in the end whether the historical or the racist conception weighs more. Let us take a look at this astonishing piece of prose:

> That he [the Jew] had lost the ground beneath his feet and had to maintain himself on a piece of borrowed earth had *its good side* and its bad side; he—*apart from a few great exceptions—had to* misuse his advantages *in order to survive* in *the contested* and groundless condition—he *mostly* misused himself and others. With a cunning that he had *learned from self-preservation*, he transformed his rootlessness *from a misfortune* into a superiority, and wherever he misused this *dearly purchased superiority* in a petty, greedy, or antagonistic way, wherever he—*involuntarily* takes revenge, there he has become a pest, an intruder, a divisive force. *However, wherever the same process, the same survival earned from destiny, was accomplished in a <u>grandly</u> determined nature, there arose out of the same inexorable conditions that magnificence for which <u>Spinoza</u> would be a famous example.* Mobility and exchangeability of the inner center, its *independence* (but at the same time rootlessness, *unless reflection leads down to the root in God*)—the spirit that is actually <u>transportable</u> has come into the world through *the destiny* of the Jew: an unheard of danger and *an unheard of freedom of movement.* And depending on whether one emphasizes the one or the *other* side of the Jewish alternative, one will have to fear or *praise* it; whereby it remains the case that that which has been effected by him

is indispensable to all of us, not to be thought away and *not to be wished away*.[96]

There follows a qualified approval of Zionism to which Rilke appends his wish that the Jews might use their recovered homeland and rootedness in order to return to their former relationship to God as it appears in the Old Testament. This version of anti-Semitism—playing off the biblical Jews against the modern, giving the dead their due and repudiating the living—is by no means Rilke's invention. Rather, it is a quite popular variety of prejudice proclaimed on into the twentieth century, even in the lecture halls of universities. In the passage quoted from Rilke's letter I have placed all the qualifications in italics. If we delete them, there remains not a portrait of the Jew, but a familiar caricature: a pest, intruder, and sower of discontent, a petty, greedy monster who abuses the advantages that he cunningly weaseled out of others.

We are, of course, entirely justified in making these deletions. For if Rilke presented himself for the sake of the Princess Thurn und Taxis as more anti-Semitic than he actually was, then we have a right to assume that in letters to a worried Jewess, who had bluntly asked him where he stood, he would check his impulses and show greater friendliness toward Jews than at less controlled times. In any case, there is nothing to prove the following claim of the recipient, Ilse Blumenthal-Weiss: "When . . . Rilke met a conscious and convinced Jewish person, then his attitude changed decisively."[97] Nor is our assertion of Rilke's anti-Semitism contradicted by the fact that he had several Jewish acquaintances and that several of his lovers were Jewish. There are plenty of examples that demonstrate the compatibility of an emotionally conditioned ideology and such personal relations.

Rilke's invectives are directed at various persons, recur again and again, and even in their more rational moments reveal traits characteristic of a racist ideology. If I nevertheless referred to him at the beginning as a "moderate" anti-Semite, it is because anti-Semitism was not an obsession with him. Unlike the racist fanatics, he did not make the Jewish question the cornerstone of his entire view of life, and in his most balanced attempts to confront the problem he developed the rudiments of an historically determined understanding of Judaism. Although he acknowledged exceptions, he was nevertheless of the opinion—upheld even vis-à-vis his "conscious and convinced" Jewish correspondent—that most Jews had abused the superiority over others that they had earned for themselves through cunning. To be a Spinoza is not given to everyone, even if it were possible to save one's life through such an ascent.

Nationalism

The retreat to the values of the nation, beginning with the honest patriot and reaching to the exalted chauvinist, the rejection of world-embracing "ism's" like humanism, cosmopolitanism and internationalism—these were typical characteristics of the European Right. Without them a fascist movement is unthinkable. The symbols of race and nation remained the final refuge of the petit bourgeois who, swallowed up by modern economic and social developments, was painfully afraid that he too might sink to the ranks of the "nationless" proletariat and be stripped of his identity by the communist leveling process.

Here, Rilke would seem at last to have an airtight alibi. A world traveler competent in several languages, the friend of artists and aristocrats from all over Europe, intimate with many literatures, and from early on permanently estranged from his own German heritage, he would seem to be immune to even the mildest attack of nationalism. The confession, "Since I've been able to think, the national has been

PERIOD OF MATURITY

infinitely distant from me,"[98] differs only by virtue of its poignancy from many similar statements in Rilke's correspondence. Still more frequent are his attempts to set himself apart from Germany and Austria as we have already seen in letters quoted earlier. In the final analysis he blamed Germany for the First World War, a judgment that emerges from his unpublished correspondence with Dr. Wilhelm Mühlon. Rilke had read Mühlon's book, *The Devastation of Europe. Notes from the First Months of the War*, written in 1914 but only published in Zürich in 1918. This work is still of interest today.

Mühlon, a far-seeing "good European," paints a most critical picture of Germany's conduct of the war on the basis of documents to which he probably had access because of his leading position in heavy industry at the outset of the war. For example: "If the Germans attain hegemony in Europe, a general exodus of Europeans will commence."[99] Or:

> ... today's Prussianism [Mühlon was Bavarian] can only bring deeper hate to the European peoples, intensifying it even to the point of obsession. It will rob whatever it can in order to hold onto it. It will only give what it cares nothing about, and that at the cost of others. It will never take its foot from the neck of the defeated or those conquered by a surprise attack. It will force every foreign civilization to honor its barbarism. It only believes in the strong fist, both within its borders and outside. It recognizes no other power on earth than physical compulsion.[100]

Mühlon attributes a higher morality to the soldiers of enemy and allied nations than to the German soldier, who knows no "pardon," who unnecessarily plunders, robs, and murders innocents and brags about it besides. He places the responsibility for this immorality with the German government and military leadership. Rilke, who had met the author in Switzerland, accords the book his complete agreement, and in so doing sharply expresses his accumulated animosity toward Germany once again.[101]

Even after 1918 Rilke continued to see in Germany the source of belligerence in Europe: "For me . . . there is no doubt that it is Germany which, by not knowing itself, holds back the world." And to this he adds: "The motley mixture and the broad education of my blood affords me a unique distance."[102] Bolder even than this assertion are the repeated allusions to his "Slavic blood," which must have rattled like a cacophony in the ear of every German nationalist. Rilke speaks of the "deeply Slavic person" that he is,[103] and ten years later his wish "that the Slavic current might not be the most negligible in the multiple mixture of my blood" remains unaltered.[104] He has no objections whatsoever to the new state of Czechoslovakia, which until its destruction was a thorn in the side of the German jingoists. Indeed, should he be classified due to his birth as a citizen of that country, he declares to his publisher, then he would quietly and politely come to terms with this fact since the composition of his nature has, after all, a good deal to thank that nation for.[105] He did even more than remain quiet: "To President Masaryk I have offered . . . my veneration. . . . This feeling existed long ago, even before the rising of the year '18 lifted him into that conspicuous place. How should I not have felt that my applause was called for, when a man of worldwide importance was given the highest place in the country of my birth, from which I am distant enough to be faithful, in an aloof way, to its particular fate?"[106] It is no wonder that that statement "occasioned ugly comments."[107] An open conflict with the alert upholders of German honor broke out when Rilke published his French poems. "Double-tongued Poet!" they raged in the German press as a consequence of this "most superfluous matter," as Rilke phrases it in a letter to Walter Mehring who had defended him in print. It is noteworthy

PERIOD OF MATURITY

that a relationship with this literary figure should develop as a result of the affair because it shows how rapidly someone who fails to toot on the nationalist trumpet is driven into the camp of the *Weltbühne*.[108]

Yet in Rilke's case things are never so simple as they seem at first glance. Perhaps his most acerbic attack on Germany is to be found in those same *Lettres Milanaises* to which we have so often referred and which at the same time voice a hymn to Mussolini that is not at all free of nationalist impulses. "The example of the German people," Rilke lectures, "would seem to have been made to render suspect every effort at deliberate nationalization."[109] He finds fault with the German's "current ambitious grimace," speaks of a "most irresponsible *abuse* of the national sentiment," calls Wilhelm II "the most hideous figure . . . in contemporary history," and characterizes the Wilhelminian empire as "unhappy, pretentious and grandiloquent," as an "abstraction of vanity and bad taste." Of himself he adds, true to the facts, that he has "always detested *German* nationalism, the pretention of a vaguely Americanized parvenu."[110] The word "German" must be stressed in this context, for the entire exchange of thoughts on fascism was set off by the following remark of Rilke's on a speech by the *duce*: "Such a beautiful discourse as the one M. Mussolini addressed to the governor of Rome!"[111] To this the countess gave her admired mentor *in poeticis* a gentle but unambiguously disapproving reply.[112]

Since Rilke's letter to the countess is dated January 5, 1926, the speech referred to must be the one given by the *duce* on December 31, 1925, on the occasion of the ceremonious installation of Senator Fillippo Cremonesi as the first *Governatore dell'Urbe*.[113] If we read this speech today, we are compelled to ask what Rilke found so appealing about it. The topics are such things as new housing developments, streets, pools, parks and athletic fields, the improvement of health care, the restoration of ruins, temples and other antiquities—all praiseworthy things, but hardly such as to explain the enthusiasm of a great metaphysical poet. If one is not satisfied in assuming that Rilke was at that time inflamed by everything that came from Mussolini, then one can continue the search further, stopping finally at the characteristic fascist rhetoric of order, heroism, and discipline introduced by the grandiose but hardly serious disavowal: "Rigorosamente esclusa ogni divagazione retorica." Could it be that slogans like "Roman style," "solemn latinity," or the call for a return "to the times of Augustus' first empire," or for a liberation of the "ancient monuments of our history" from the "centuries of decadence"—could it be that such grandiloquence stirred the heart of the Schuler admirer Rilke?[114] Perhaps it was the pompous patriotic cadence that concludes Mussolini's speech by evoking the "greater Rome that will arise from our efforts, our tenacious will, from the conscious, the consenting love and sacrifice of all the peoples of Italy?" This is how it must have been. The dream of Latin and Roman grandeur was, as historians have taught us, something that ghosted about in many brains of the period.[115] We turn the pages and find confirmation of our hypothesis from Rilke's own pen. In the *Lettres Milanaises*, Rilke repeats Mussolini's slogans[116] as if they were his own formulations. We hear of the "Roman idea" and of the "unity sensed and assented to," which is doubtlessly intended as a translation of "concorde e consapevole." And then the eager pupil continues entirely in the tone of the great master: "It is this glorious past, the giant vestiges of which your soil still carries, that makes possible this architect of the Italian will, this smith forging a consciousness that blazes up anew at the flames of an ancient fire. Happy Italy!"[117]

There are then two nationalisms: a despised German variety and a Roman variety that receives approval. Whoever remains sceptical should listen to the verbal fanfare summoned up by our former pupil of the royal and imperial cadet schools—he who had seemed so deeply offended in his sensibilities: "Although it would have been difficult for me elsewhere, in these countries I could have been, with conviction and enthusiasm, a soldier, had I been born there: an Italian soldier, a French soldier, yes, I could have been that, fraternally, to the point of the ultimate sacrifice."[118] One could interpret this as infantile regression on Rilke's part, for as early as 1892 he had expressed similar sentiments in a poem against Berta von Suttner:

> What noble men of all times considered
> the highest, most beautiful payment for their striving
> was to do battle and strife for the fatherland,
> as a whole man and as a faithful son.
> ....
> So hold tight to the sabre in your right hand,
> never let it sink from your grip,
> and call out danger, *then* be prepared to fight,
> prepared to die for the fatherland.[119]

Dulce et decorum est pro patria mori! The fatherlands have changed but the yearning for a sacrificial death has remained.[120] And yet, near the end of life one is not entirely as naïve as at the beginning. Now the explanation is that for some peoples nationalism is good, for others inappropriate: "The national question is one of the thorniest there is. It is not the same, it seems to me, for all peoples."[121]

Another passage in the *Lettres Milanaises* deserves especially close attention: "I think that every people has to have had some of these brusquely nationalist moments in order to form its self-consciousness or quite simply in order to know itself. It is not by cultivating a vague internationalism that peoples will best come closer. . . . " Indeed, even "nationalist fury" is spoken of entirely positively.[122] When we read: "In order that we might one day (which I believe to be still far off) reach an unforseeable

European concord, it will be necessary that the different countries advance (in the interim) along diverse paths,"[123] then we believe we are hearing de Gaulle with his "Europe des patries."

If we analyze Rilke's statements about Germany from this point of view, we discover a further dimension previously overlooked. What Rilke finds lacking in contemporary Germany is the lost agrarian idyll of ages past, the "charming and a bit old-fashioned and 'provincial' qualities of these German principalities with their slow and particular ways." But Rilke goes further still: "It is necessary to return to the drawings of Albrecht Dürer and the old masters in order to rediscover the true German figure; one of his essential traits was this hard and durable humility of the rustic and rural people. . . . "[124] Here Rilke has succumbed to the illusion of many conservatives who believed that fascism would turn back the wheel of history, reverse the processes of industrialism and capitalism, undo the French Revolution, and lead back to the world of simple virtues that characterized ancient Rome[125] and the German Middle Ages, the peasant and village paradise of the *ancien régime*.

The mention of Dürer's name is not an arbitrary allusion to an old master, but rather the rallying cry of social conservatives from Langbehn to Eugen Diederichs.[126] We already encountered the name in the letter where Rilke claimed Germany was holding back the world. He had hoped, Rilke says there, that after the war "the lost trait of that humility, which strikes one as such a constructive element in Dürer's drawings, would be etched, re-etched in the German physiognomy which has become so strangely one-sided and willful." Now we can better understand the nature of this humility and what Rilke expects from the Germans: "a determined renunciation of their falsely developed prosperity."

> Germany has missed the opportunity to give its purest and finest measure reestablished on the oldest foundation—it

PERIOD OF MATURITY

has not renewed and reflected on itself from the ground up, it has not created that dignity, which has innermost humility as its root, it was only concerned with saving itself in a superficial, rash, mistrusting and profit-hungry sense, it wanted to perform and to get ahead and to get away instead of, as would be appropriate to its most intimate nature, bearing the burden, holding out and being prepared for its miracle.[127]

What we previously considered as vague and, for that reason, hardly comprehensible ideas has now become transparent. Rilke castigated Germany on account of its capitalism; "profit-hungry" is the key word. This is no doubt the reason why he did not grant Germany the "brusque" nationalism that he accorded to, indeed, even prescribed for other countries. Should a regime that, like the Italian leadership, preached the Catonian virtues of the simple life, discipline, and order have come to power in Germany, who knows, perhaps he would then have overcome his anti-Prussian prejudices and allowed for a Germanic patriotism alongside the Roman variety. The necessary elements were all there: a new will to harshness,[128] the insistence on civil peace and order at any cost,[129] satiation with freedom,[130] disdain for democratic parliamentary procedures and institutions,[131] disgust with material profit,[132] soldierly preparedness,[133] and a new, "mysterious" concept of the nation.[134]

Chapter 5
Lyric Poetry and Politics

Our analysis up to this point has demonstrated that Rilke's inner participation in the socio-political developments of his age was more profound than is usually assumed. Now, however, we must inquire whether our second premise is equally valid, namely that the political stance of an author within the social circumstances of his time leaves a recognizable trace in his works, be it consciously or unconsciously. To be sure, we have already seen that such products of Rilke's imagination as *Two Stories of Prague*, the *Stories of Our Dear Lord*, the *Notebooks of Malte Laurids Brigge* and the *Book of Hours* amply satisfy this condition. But the first two of these are youthful works that remain unrefined precisely to the degree that they express all too directly the poet's own troubled situation. And the two more mature works were only referred to peripherally in order to illustrate certain general principles. No one, of course, would deny that the "Five Songs" composed in 1924 by the nearly forty-year-old poet consists of anything but the poet's confrontation with a concrete historical conflict, the First World War. Yet even this result must be deemed insufficient. These poems can at best be compared to those works of a composer that are somewhat condescendingly treated as program music. Their single and avowed purpose is precisely to free the artist from the burden of impressions that force themselves upon his spirit. The consequence of this type of poetic production is that the poet characteristically rejects the work as soon as he has found through his writing some sort of resolution to the problem that instigated it in the first place. Much the same can be said, by the way, of the *Two Stories of Prague*.

The task, therefore, is to search for traces of actual social conditions in a work that the poet himself considered central to his poetic mission. To the degree that such traces can be discovered at all, their significance for the writer's entire *oeuvre* is likewise to be determined. To put it another way: we must analyze the socio-historical dimension of a well-known work, showing how it reaches into those spheres of Rilke's thought which we have investigated up to this point.

In order to be completely fair to ourselves, we must point out that merely the choice of an esoteric lyric poet like Rilke makes the exposure of such social factors extremely difficult. The work of a novelist, no matter how apolitical he might claim to be, is tied to historical reality by innumerable visible threads and would therefore provide much less resistance to our particular undertaking.[1] Our difficulties are then compounded by the fact that we have placed the *Duino Elegies*, supplemented by a few of the *Sonnets to Orpheus*, at the center of our inquiry. We are dealing, in other words, with a poetry so sublime that not only the poet but also most of his exegetes would consider it a sacrilege to associate such verse with politics. But if we can show that even these poems, which seem so remote from political reality, are connected with politics, then we will have made a strong case for the more general axiom that politics and literature are always intertwined.

The *Duino Elegies* are considered the crowning achievement of Rilke's entire work. This estimation echoes that of the poet, who prepared himself for the *Elegies* for over a decade, wrote them down during a stormy period of creation that lasted only a few weeks, and then proclaimed to the world that he had accomplished what was most truly given him to do. Even if one claims to find in the poems of his last years, composed mainly in French, a new style and a self-sufficient phase of poetic development,[2] the cycle of ten elegies nevertheless remains a central monument in which Rilke's image of man and the world has achieved an authentic form. We shall in any case keep them before us as we attempt to unite the seemingly incongruent domains of his poetry on the one hand and on the other his everyday concerns.

The *Elegies* begin with the famous question: "And if I cried, who'd listen to me...?"[3] which strikes one, in view of our investigation thus far, as quite characteristic. An 'I' struggles to express a solitude that has been intensified to the point of unbearable torture. But the outcry of protest considered here remains purely hypothetical. A series of subjunctive clauses makes clear that the line has already been crossed and the creature-like utterance of one's torment no longer has meaning, no longer provides spiritual illumination.

The other pole, the highest authority which the powerless 'I' of the *Elegies* faces, is the angel, a fictional figure who has already overcome the world of concrete phenomena which causes the 'I' to suffer so. In the angel, the rebellion against empirical conditions, which was a theme of the worker's letter written contemporaneously with the *Elegies*, has been transformed into pure, unprotesting inwardness.[4] "The angel of the *Elegies*," Rilke explains to his Polish translator, "is that creature in whom the transformation of the visible into the invisible ... appears as already accomplished."[5]

We will not concern ourselves here with such questions as have so productively stimulated the scholastics of Rilke research: what the angel actually is, whether Rilke meant it as a symbol or believed in its existence, whether it corresponds to Christian angels, which Rilke denies, or whether it is similar to the angels of Islam as he suggests.[6] For our purposes it is merely important to keep in mind that the angel, the sole authority in the *Elegies*, shows in its perfection neither care nor concern for mankind. On the contrary, not unlike the authorities of another Prague writer, Kafka, Rilke's angel remains infinitely distant from man, unreachable. So uncanny and overwhelming is the angel that closer contact with it could not even be wished for, indeed it would lead to the destruction of the individual. Of necessity, then, the 'I' decides to suppress the cry he had hardly begun: "So I control myself and choke back the lure/ of my dark cry."[7] What in Goethe's works once brought salvation to the tormented individual—namely to say what he is suffering—has in the twentieth century become altogether senseless.

The outcry can be suppressed, but not the despair. What follows next is a gripping account of human solitude, of a total estrangement in which man, gradually disowned by all the creatures, must finally recognize that he no longer has a relationship to anything else in the world. Even an individual's habits have become self-sufficient personifications who can choose at their own discretion whether or not to remain attached to a person. Isolation has been intensified to the point of reification and schizophrenia. Rilke summarizes this misery in the litotes: "we're not comfortably at home/ in our interpreted world."[8] This pronouncement with its ironic understatement is clear and we can recognize its applicability to our daily experience. Only the word "interpreted" is ambiguous and difficult. It becomes more comprehensible if we gauge it against its implicit opposites. On the one hand, an interpreted world stands in opposition to a world that is known; on the other hand, it is opposed to a world that is directly experienced. Both meanings unite in their consequences to express the enormous distance between man and his surroundings and the disturbance of his natural relationship to life.[9] As regards this one aspect, the unquestioned meaningfulness of existence, all the various creatures of the *Elegies*—the angels, the many plants and animals, indeed even the lifeless doll—seem to be preferable to man. And so he whom everything excludes remains thrown back entirely on himself.

This is the basic situation of the elegies, the fundamental melody evoked and nuanced in a variety of ways and varied through every possible major and minor key. In the "Ninth Elegy," for instance, the question is formulated in a different manner: what is the meaning of human life when compared with that of the plants? In the "Eighth Elegy" it is the animal that serves as a contrast. The "Fifth Elegy" introduces the troupers, the *saltimbanquis*, as an emblem of mankind. Their homeless moving about and their empty performances before the eyes of the world are only a slightly intensified representation of a general homelessness, a representation which has the advantage that it more distinctly profiles the highest law of human life. "And we: spectators, always, everywhere," the "Eighth Elegy" says. "We arrange it. It decays./ We arrange it again and we decay."[10] The perspectives shift; the central fact remains unchanged.

If life is transient and no recognizable sense can be wrung from this transience, then death too becomes questionable. This explains why the effort to fill time and to find a proper relationship to death occupies so much space in the *Elegies*. The crassest senselessness, however, resides in the death of young people who have not had time even to try out the possibilities inherent in life. Thus, their all too early dying becomes a problem that Rilke wants to solve in order not to have to consign human existence to an absolute meaninglessness. Out of this justification grows the *cult* of the dead, so definitive for the late Rilke, that quite possibly derives from Alfred Schuler while exhibiting many features of the earth and death mysticism so often encountered in European rightest movements.

Let us depart from the *Elegies* themselves for a moment in order to explore this point a bit further. In 1915, Rilke met Alfred Schuler and heard the third and fourth lectures in a series then being given by the independent scholar. This was the lecture on "Caena and Thermal Baths."[11] Rilke missed the other lectures at first but later, on the occasion of a repeat performance in 1919, managed to attend them as well.[12] That he was deeply impressed by Schuler can be inferred from several statements in letters.[13] From the very beginning, what fascinated Rilke above all was Schuler's mystical interpretation of death: "Imagine that a person, starting from an intuitive insight into ancient imperial Rome, undertook to provide an explanation of the world that presents the dead as the authentically being, the realm of the dead as a unified, unheard-of state of existence from which our own little term of life is but a kind of exception. . . ."[14] Rilke himself recognized Schuler's influence on his poetry: "In the *Sonnets to Orpheus* there is a good deal that Schuler would have acknowledged too; indeed, who knows whether stating some of it so openly and at the same time so secretly doesn't come from the contact with him."[15] Even a superficial look at Schuler's lectures, the third for example, reveals surprising correspondences to typical Rilkean notions. I quote here randomly some of the more astonishing passages:

> Everywhere we observe the development of pomp and splendor in the past there lies hidden a mystery of the inner world. . . . The rose is of all flowers the most quintessential, the symbol most inner to life. . . . The ceremony that presents the innermost kernel of the *caena romana*, namely the prayer to the Lares, the prayer to the ancestors. . . . Dolls are only symbols of the soul. . . . Beyond this I must . . . point out that on all the Etruscan ash vases the dead person

or his wife are lying, are thought of as lying at the caena...."[16]

In order to place all this in the context most relevant to our inquiry it is not sufficient merely to repeat the claim that Schuler was a "pre-fascist anti-Semite."[17] Still, that we are dealing here with a genuine problem about which Rilke criticism has little or nothing informative to say can be inferred from the prominence of the death cult among the European rightest movements. I quote here merely one passage from Eugen Weber's introduction: "The nationalist usually couples this impersonal mana with the animistic vision of something primitive societies also know very well: *la terre et les morts*—a world animated and dynamized by ancestral spirits and traditions. Out of this conjunction he produces a new religion, celebrating both mana and ancestors as sources of social energy for national revival, reform, and self-assertion."[18]

These observations throw an interesting new light on several passages in the *Elegies* and especially in the *Sonnets to Orpheus*, for instance the following:

First Part, 14

We're involved with flower, fruit, grapevine.
They speak more than the language of the year.
Out of the darkness a blaze of colors appears,
and one perhaps that has the jealous shine

of the dead, those who strengthen the earth.
What do we know of the part they assume?
It's long been their habit to marrow the loam
with their own free marrow through and through.

Now the one question: Is it done gladly?
The work of sullen slaves, does the fruit
thrust up, clenched, toward us, its masters?

Sleeping with roots, granting us only
out of their surplus this hybrid made of mute
strength and kisses—are they the masters?[19]

Schuler was very much influenced by Bachofen and it is this writer who forms the link between Schuler's world and Rilke. "And indeed almost the whole symbolism of Rilke's late poetry stems from Bachofen, mainly from his later work on 'Orphic Theology.'"[20]

Returning now to the *Elegies*, we must emphasize that the concretization of the problem of death in terms of personifications is not at all an isolated phenomenon. It is among the most important presentational modes in the *Elegies*. For what Rilke undertakes here is an exploration of the possibilities of earthly life through a series of such figurative embodiments. He parades before the reader, in the form of nearly mythic characters, various exemplary forms of human existence that have traditionally been considered especially meaningful or sublime. He questions each as to the purpose of life: the child, the hero, the saints, the lovers. One after the other, they are summoned forth and are asked to show us how the terrible fragility and the oppressive loneliness of existence might be overcome. The many when's, who's and why's are the rhetorical mirroring of this questioning and uncertainty.

Four of the ten elegies begin with important questions bearing on the central problematics of human life, and a large number of question marks are scattered elsewhere throughout the text as well. The answer however is again and again the same: although Rilke never tires in his praise of the earthly magnificence of these figures, not a single one of them is found to be sufficient to justify human existence and to break through man's absolute solitude. Even the lovers, those figures Rilke doubtlessly admired most— an abandoned lover, after all, stands at least knee-high to an angel[21]—even they merely occlude from one another the destiny to which all mankind is condemned. Perhaps we should add to these almost mythic figures that of the poet, who, despite the fact he never appears personally on the poem's stage, is nevertheless always present as the principal and most eloquent advocate of man. To the degree that any sort of solution is offered in the *Elegies*, it is the poet's task to undertake the attempt to redeem human existence.

Is it arbitrary or whimsical to relate this basic experience, in which the isolation and senselessness of human life have been elevated almost to a cosmic principle, to the anomie of the technological age, a thoroughly historical concept? Even if Rilke spoke of nothing else, even if he presented this isolation and senselessness as an unalterable *condition humaine*, a condition that is always and everywhere inseparably associated with human existence, even then one could still conceive of this as an abstraction, as the hypostasis of a historically specific, subjective experience. For if nothing else, Rilke's way of speaking is at least entirely modern and the historian knows that in any other age he would have written differently. Perhaps, indeed in all likelihood, loneliness is a condition inseparable from man's existence. What is peculiarly modern, however, is that man becomes ever more acutely aware of this. Odysseus clinging to his plank in the middle of the sea, Robinson Crusoe rebuilding his life on a remote island—neither felt as lonely as Dostoevsky's characters in Petersburg or as Rilke's Malte in Paris. But we need not rely on mere speculations here. The *Duino Elegies* themselves draw much more explicitly, tightly, and convincingly the connection between Rilke's existential despair and phenomena long since recognized in the historical disciplines.

To be sure, the wanderings through the realm of the laments, across a world that the angels ignore perhaps but nevertheless rule, the appearance of mystical constellations in the nights "full of world-space,"[22] the earth inhabited by silent plants and animals—all that could not be presented in a more timeless fashion. And the representations of the various anthropological conditions—father, mother, child, the recently dead, the heroes and lovers, indeed even the members of definite professional groups such as the circus

LYRIC POETRY AND POLITICS

people, the potters and rope-makers—could hardly have been selected more ahistorically. Nevertheless, man in the *Elegies* is an historical being and his situation is consciously viewed historically. For a long time the rhythms flow along, bearing their vocabulary of sheerly unreachable spheres—"shields of ecstasy,"[23] "state of timeless serenity"[24]—suggesting eternally human conditions unaffected by any temporal change or earthly misery. But in a few passages this timeless existential view reverses itself, an historical element erupts into the text and imprints itself upon the entire work. It turns out that Rilke is intentionally giving form here to a concrete historical experience.

What first attracts one's attention to this are certain temporal modifiers, as in the "Seventh Elegy": "And ever more the outer world vanishes."[25] Or in the "Ninth Elegy," where the lament is raised: "The things/ we can live with are falling away more/ than ever, . . ."[26] It requires no particular acumen to figure out that magnitudes existing next to one another in space are *not* being compared here. The intention of these comparatives is rather to point to the progressive deterioration of social conditions, to contrast two temporal planes with one another, one in which life was still characterized by fulfillment with another in which it threatens to become meaningless. That, however, is what is called thinking historically.

Rilke did not have much of an historical sense and one of his most intelligent friends even remarked: "Rilke lacked any feeling whatsoever for the idea of the historical."[27] The poet himself recognized this weakness and on one occasion he speaks about it in a letter: "I am puzzling . . . about the common future of us all although I have to rely in doing so on fewer premises than some onlooker since history is so obscure to me."[28] Rilke was also aware of the historical component of all poetry but felt that he, due to his nature, was compelled to emphasize the timeless: "Would we understand such poems otherwise if they had only been the utterances of a future dead person? Don't they speak constantly to something unlimited and unknowable in us, something beyond the here and now. Yes, I think that spirit can never make itself so small that it would only affect our temporal and present part: wherever it rushes up against us, at that point we are the dead and the living in one."[29] All this, however, cannot mean that Rilke was entirely unhistorical—an impossibility in the age of historicism—and indeed we have already run up against the beginnings of an historical approach in his works.[30] In any case, we have good reason to pay especially strict attention when Rilke sets about delineating his view of history.

What aspects of the present then did he regard critically? What changes had history brought so that what Rilke was fond of seemed threatened and what he feared seemed about to triumph? Of course, we already know the answers to these questions but we must now seek them out in the form they assume in the *Elegies*. Beyond the several allusions strewn throughout the cycle, it is primarily in three segments—in the Seventh, Ninth and Tenth Elegies—that Rilke raises his accusation. All these passages are related but emphasize various aspects of Rilke's critique of the age. Taken together, and strengthened by several of the *Sonnets to Orpheus*, they constitute the historical system of coordinates of Rilke's late lyric poetry. In other poems this problematic recedes into the background. Of course, this element in the two great cycles has been noticed and, like every word in the *Elegies*, repeatedly commented on, but it has seldom been placed in the precise context we are developing here.[31] The relevant passage in the "Seventh Elegy" reads as follows:

>   Where a sturdy house
> once stood, a fantastic structure rises into view, as much
> at ease among concepts as if it still stood in the brain.
> The Zeitgeist builds huge warehouses of power, formless
> as the straining urge from which it draws all else.

Temples it can't recognize anymore. Now we're saving
these extravagances of the heart secretly. Yes, even where
one single thing that was prayed to, served, and knelt to
once, survives, it endures just as it is, in the invisible.
Many don't see it anymore and miss the chance to build
                                      it again,
complete with pillars and statues, greater than ever,
                                                within.[32]

An industrial site, probably an electrical plant, is presented here as a construction typical of the present.[33] The associations that result from this are manifold, but two qualities are especially emphasized: rationality and the elimination of symbolic value. These are the same principles that the Romantics objected to in the Enlightenment and it is therefore not at all surprising that Rilke continues their battle against the eighteenth century.[34] Modern buildings are a matter of arbitrary design, "fantastic," not to be distinguished from "concepts" because they have no tradition and could have been otherwise according to their particular function. In addition, the modern way of building—and building is merely symptomatic of every other activity—is "formless," it lacks the participation of human feeling. The temples that were typical of earlier, better times were places of devotion. Themselves the products of pious artistic activity, they were capable of providing shelter for other types of artworks. The numinous, the aesthetic, and the honorable combined in this "once" with the human need to form a beneficient unity. Modern civilization is antagonistic to art, without feeling, without a sense of respect and solely oriented toward the utilitarian subjugation of nature. The sad site of this civilization is the city whose most prominent characteristics are transience and estrangement, the ephemeral and alien city in contrast to the splendors of greater epochs: pillars, columns, sphinxes, and cathedrals.[35]

    To the two ages there also correspond two opposed types of human beings: the modern type has no sense for the nature and value of the old things and artifacts. Not only does modern man no longer build temples or create analogous things,[36] when he comes across such things from ancient times he lacks any understanding of their true significance. He spiritualizes nothing at all and therefore he fails in the authentic task that is given to human beings. Nevertheless, there still remain some representatives of another type. The underlined "*us*" in the following passage: "This/ shouldn't confuse *us*"[37] clearly distinguishes the initiates and those in the know, the conservatives, who still have a sense of the ancient ways, from the numberless incarnations of modern mass man. The entire conflict between the old and the new can be subsumed under the opposition of heart and brain which the quoted passage explicitly evokes.

The "Ninth Elegy" shows us what role these select few (the "poetic," Eichendorff would have said), with whom the poet identifies through the use of the first person plural pronoun, are to play in the overcoming of modernity. The critical points made in this elegy are not particularly new. Once again the anti-Platonic, formless aspects of modernity are railed at. These are an "action without image."[38] Once again the traditionlessness of the modern means of production, possibly of the modern mode of experience in general, is spoken of. Whether the "hammers" that the "heart"[39] must assert itself against refers to technology and factory production[40] we leave as an open question. That machinery and technical apparatuses occupied the foreground of Rilke's thought during this narrowly circumscribed period of poetic creativity can be inferred from a whole series of the *Sonnets to Orpheus*, for instance sonnets 18, 22, 23, and 24 of the first part and sonnet 10 of the second part. And the sonnet "O the new, friends," originally conceived as part of the Orpheus cycle but later published separately, likewise shows that Rilke found at this time much that was offensive to him in the world of machines.[41] All these poems are in part or entirely dedicated to a confrontation and coming to terms with technology whether manifested in the form of airplane, skyscraper, or cable. Rilke's feelings about machines are in no way complex. The tercet

> See, the Machine:
> how it spins and wreaks
> revenge, deforms and demeans us.[42]

affords us an entirely adequate account of his attitude. The most beautiful, just, and accomplished verses on the machine are those Rilke wrote in the tenth sonnet of the cycle's second part. The admonitory sadness of the opening lines

> As long as it dares to exist as spirit instead of obeying,
> the machine threatens everything we've gained.[43]

will satisfy thoughtful individuals of the most diverse political orientations and world views. And whoever during Rilke's time might have expected more from technology than the poet himself would nevertheless—given the things we have learned in our day—have to agree with him when he laments:

> It is life—it believes it's all-knowing,
> and with the same mind makes and orders and destructs.[44]

New perspectives are opened up in the "Tenth Elegy," which has less to do with technology itself than with its sociological effects. The "*City* of Pain"[45] becomes the symbolic locus of all the negative phenomena of modernity. Once again the primary attributes of the city are estrangement and—nothing has changed since the *Book of Hours*—falseness: the noise that drowns out everything authentic, the mendacious monuments, the total spiritual emptiness, the ostentatious, "glittering"[46] ornamentation. Opposed in no way to all this, but rather its most important component is the institutionalized, thoughtlessly accepted church (comparable to the state-supported post office), "bought ready-made"[47] and consequently simply another factory-produced article of the machine world.

The metropolitan civilization is extended to the "fair"[48] set up at the city's rim. This fair is presented separately probably because here the actual driving forces of this bungled urban life are held up for ridicule: the aspirations of the social reformers as "swings of freedom,"[49] the supposedly more radical agitators and revolutionaries as "high-divers and jugglers of zeal,"[50] the quest for a banal, prettified happiness in the "lifelike shooting galleries" with their "targets tumbling off the rack of tin/ when a good-shot hits once,"[51] and finally, in the "billboards plastered with posters of 'Deathless,'/ the bitter beer,"[52] the advertisement-hungry ideology of the average man euphemistically avoiding every possible tragic sense of life. Money, however, is the element that spurs all this on, the anatomical, sexual reproduction and multiplication of which is exhibited appropriately enough in obscene peep shows. The whole spectacle culminates in a splendid satire of the trivial culture of mass society.[53]

To be sure, the intellectual content here is not new, either for Rilke or for the tradition of philosophical and scientific cultural criticism, which in the course of the nineteenth century had formulated virtually every component of the poet's accusations. However, it is significant and, for our purposes, particularly noteworthy that we find the same critical ideas, in part expressed with a similar vocabulary, in Rilke's profascist letters, the *Lettres Milanaises*. We need not be over-concerned with the differences between the world-famous *Duino Elegies*, composed in a high poetic idiom developed and intensified through the centuries, and these letters accidentally provoked by the revulsion felt by a young Italian woman vis-à-vis fascism and written in the French patois of the international high society. The monumental poetic work and the letters are twin phenomena in spirit, not in form. The one is imagistic and synthetic, the other intellectual and analytic; they relate to one another as an historical myth to a theory of history. That the poems offer inwardness, the letters fascism as the cure for the illnesses of the age need not imply a contradiction as Thomas Mann's well-known formula "power-protected inwardness" reveals. At the same time, the individual correspondences between the *Elegies* and the *Lettres Milanaises* are so numerous and convincing that the world view of the *Elegies* of 1922 (indeed, in part from 1912, when important parts were first conceived) must be considered as having remained valid until 1926, the year of the poet's death in which the two long political letters were written to the duchess.

In the *Lettres Milanaises* it is likewise the triad money, technology, and freedom[54] against which Rilke directs his attack. First there is the quest for profit[55] and the centrality of money which has become the chief symbol of modern life suppressing everything else.[56] Then follows the untiring, indifferent machine with its common products and by-products, conceived without love by an inventiveness that takes nothing but profit into its calculations.[57] Rilke's most ardently waged campaign, however, is aimed at freedom, that same freedom which in the *Elegies* is consigned to the secondhand market of the City of Pain. It is freedom that causes the world's ills; freedom is the phantom that leads even the finest intellects astray;[58] it is freedom that culminates in an empty and inane parliamentarianism.[59] Bolshevism shows us where the path of freedom eventually leads![60] And why? Because freedom cleaves to the rational and never gets man any further than what he understands, the narrowly circumscribed domain of his reason.[61] Even for great, truly idealistic minds freedom poses a danger. If it gets control of mediocre brains and short-sighted men of action, then it ends in that empty democracy and profit mania, that system of terrible injustices that boasts of having done away with the old injustices, although these were in fact so much more innocent. These attacks on liberalism could be supplemented by certain passages from the *Sonnets to Orpheus*, for instance the ninth sonnet of the second part where the modern advocates of gradual reform are assailed as follows:

> Judges, don't boast because you've abolished torture,
> and the neck's no longer shackled by iron.
> Because a planned spasm of mercy twists you more
> tenderly—no heart's elated, not one.[62]

And in the eleventh sonnet of the second part, hunting is given explicit approbation: "Let every breath of pity be far from witnesses. . . ." The philosophical insight that follows from this, however, is emphasized by the poet through the use of italics:

> *Killing's one shape of our restless affliction.* . . .[63]

The opposite side of freedom, the submission to commands, even to brutality, occupies a good deal of space in the *Lettres Milanaises*. What is required according to Rilke is not freedom but "a proud, voluntary obedience"[64] and a "curative, sure violence," a principle which "true dictators at times have understood very well."[65] "One would do nature injustice were one to consider her slow and forgiving: how much violence after all has taken place in her innocent womb!"[66]

Despite the predominance of socio-political factors in these reflections, Rilke nevertheless does not entirely neglect their application to poetry: in life as in art a certain violence is necessary in order to create order; even where it is applied brutally it has something of the innocence of nature.[67] Even at the risk of astonishing his correspondent, he, Rilke, must unconditionally reject a good-willed, "humane" poetry. In politics and in poetry deliberately humane impulses would be altogether worthless, for one knows so little about good and evil. What is essential is not the desire to help or to comfort but rather obedience to an authoritarian dictate.[68]

Rilke, of course, by no means stands alone in this translation of certain principles relevant to poetry into the language of social and political issues. Let us note what John R. Harrison has to say about the "reactionaries" among the English-speaking poets: "They based their political and social criticism on the same principles as their imaginative writing and literary criticism. They transferred their value-judgments from aesthetics to politics. . . . The desire for 'classical' order, discipline, strict rules and hardness in literature led Yeats, Pound, Lewis and Eliot to demand the same in society."[69] Needless to say, it would be possible to argue the other way around and to seek the fundamental nature of these views in the political and social spheres. Then it would not be a matter of the poets borrowing aesthetic principles in order to improve *society* but rather of their insisting on a specific social organization in order to secure their position as *poets*. Harrison hints at this as well:

> There were those people, particularly the literary intelligentsia, who saw the problem as essentially a cultural one. Confronted with cheap national newspapers, radio, films, they thought they saw a massive decline in cultural standards and attributed this to the spread of democracy. Fascism, violently antidemocratic, also seemed to them to be a modern counterpart of earlier hierarchic societies in which authority, stability and inequality had provided the soil of flourishing artistic cultures.[70]

As some writers, for instance Thomas Mann, believed, there existed yet another relationship between poetry and fascism, a magical one. Eugen Weber has pointed this out:

> In this sense the radical leader, not the fascist alone, is very much the possessed servant of the myth he handles at his peril, as all witches do. He is also a poet in the Greek sense, where poetry is quite literally make-believe and carries ominous overtones: 'For the craft of the poet,' Plato tells us, 'is light and winged and holy and he is not capable of poetry until he is inspired and out of his mind, and there is no reason in him. Until he gets into this state, any man is powerless to produce poetry and to prophesy.' But it is worth remembering that from Plato's *Republic* such poets were excluded. They were tricksters and, their influence must prove socially subversive: 'Strip what the poet has to say of its poetical coloring, and I think you must have seen what it comes to in plain prose. It is like a face which was never really handsome, when it has lost the fresh bloom of youth.'[71]

Naturally, such statements on Rilke's part go much further than the *Elegies*. But nothing in the *Elegies* contradicts their thrust; it is, so to speak, implicit in them. This becomes especially clear—and this is doubtless the most astonishing similarity—when we consider that in both, the Milan letters and the *Duino Elegies*, not only the negative element, the critique of the world situation, is the same, but also the positive doctrine: that is, the transformation of the visible into the invisible which, both poetically and politically, constitutes the very center of Rilke's world view. This doctrine is formulated so clearly in the *Lettres Milanaises* and is provided with such concrete and poignant illustrations that these letters deserve to be placed alongside that much more famous letter of November 13, 1925, to Witold von Hulewics, as an aid in the interpretation of the *Elegies*. Now we wish to begin an attempt to explicate certain problematic passages in the *Elegies* through reference to parallel passages in the letters to Signora Gallarati-Scotti.

How does the sensitive person conduct himself in a

LYRIC POETRY AND POLITICS

world that risks being vulgarized by money, rendered degenerate by freedom, and destroyed by the machine? The "Seventh Elegy" proclaims: "... The World exists nowhere but within"[72] and insinuates that we must "build it ... within."[73] The "Ninth Elegy" struggles forward to the demand that, as far as the things of the world are concerned, we "change them completely in our invisible hearts" because what the earth ultimately wants is "to resurrect/ in us invisibly."[74] Whoever doesn't understand what this might mean can turn to the *Lettres Milanaises* for background information. During the Middle Ages and up to the eighteenth century, life was uniquely "real."[75] "Real" is a term that also occurs in the "Tenth Elegy" where, right after leaving the fair, we enter the "real": "Children are playing, to one side lovers are holding each other,/ earnest in the thinning grass, and dogs are doing nature's bidding."[76] Apparently "real" means natural, meaningful, uncomplicated.

But the *Lettres Milanaises* help us go further: the crafts and the accomplishments, the destinies, the feelings, even the most secret inner impulses, everything "reached a sort of realization, became visible and almost graspable."[77] There are many parallels to this in the *Elegies*, where "visible" and "invisible" constitute an important opposition. The world and society ought to be visible so that the poet who has truly comprehended his task can take them into his inwardness and preserve them there, that is to say, make them invisible. If, as our analysis of the *Elegies* has shown, the product is *formless* even at the time of its origination, if in other words it is invisible—and this is the case according to Rilke—then culture has ceased to exist and the mission of the poet has also become superfluous. Unless, of course, he attends to the old, to what has been left over from more fruitful epochs.

The *Lettres Milanaises* explain historically, as no other passage in Rilke's entire *oeuvre* does, why everything was so beautiful and simple and visible before the industrial revolution or the French Revolution—for what else could have had such a disruptive effect in the eighteenth century?—made things so incurably complicated:

> A highly personal pain by no means found it sufficient to transform inwardly the affected person: one *saw* a glorious knight join a particular order or a noble lady disappear behind the veil of a nun. Pride and noble wealth *realized* themselves in the mass of palaces and castles while humble belief, the most devoted misery and eternally human despair joined together in order to erect the testimony and the pious challenge of the cathedrals through the hands of countless craftsmen. Everything worked together to expand the realm of the *visible*. Even the money in the chests and trunks was heavy with all its metallic weight which it still had from the mountains.
>
> And today? Today exactly the opposite is the case. While before everything became the most real and most secure substantial material so that the spirit could settle down there without fear and even in the midst of catastrophes could move from one thing to another, today everything has become airy and floating, the events that affect us the most renounce *visibility*, material catastrophes have suppressed almost everywhere the spirit-laden events. Now the machine represents the *visible*, floods the world with its products aimed solely at profit whereby the vital human meaning of a thing is not even taken into consideration.[78]

Now we can better understand what was meant in the *Elegies* with statements like: "And ever more the outer world vanishes." or: "The things/ we can live with are falling away more/ than ever. . . ."[79]

How then does one get out of this satanic circle? How does one instill the children with a sense of goodness and love in an evil, heartless world? In a society that produces in order to live, how does one educate the young for that other, authentic existence in which the individual lives in order to produce?[80] The *Lettres Milanaises* believe fascism capable of pulling off this trick. Here the historical-mythological and, as it were, metaphysical aspects of Rilke's preference for fascism coincide with his admiration for the practical accomplishments of the Mussolini regime. The practical side of Rilke's views is quite apparently due to the influence of Gonzague de Reynold whose essay on fascism, in the *Figaro* of January 14, 1926, Rilke cuts out and sends to the Duchess. The article discusses the economic situation in Europe which it claims is everywhere worse than in 1924, except in Italy where, thanks to fascism, people are working. Then Reynold lists the reasons which in his view have brought about this advantageous state of affairs: tranquility and order, tax relief, the elimination of bureaucratic arbitrariness, freedom from the fear of strikes and revolutions. In comparison to these advantages, certain other phenomena don't seem to count at all for Reynold: neither the somewhat brutal way of governing, nor the strangulation of the press, nor the muzzling of the opposition. All of Europe, then, must either accept fascism or go under.[81]

Faithful echoes of these views can be found in Rilke's writings. The author of the article, the father-in-law of Carl Burckhardt, was a respected person for Rilke simply because of his friendship with the family. In addition, as author of the book *Cités et pays suisses*, which always occupied a place on the table in the anteroom at Muzot, Reynold was both well-known to and admired by Rilke. The only thing about Reynold that he criticized was his Catholicism, which however plays no explicit role in the article. Otherwise, Rilke's economic ideas are carbon copies of Reynold's, for instance when he writes: "In any case this Italy of 1926 admirably exhibits vitality and a strong will while the disarray that continues in the surrounding countries undermines them and works toward their destruction. This is a fact to which, in the meantime, I would not hesitate to sacrifice a few ideas and a few feelings, so great and impatient is my desire for order."[82]

The *Elegies* offer a different answer to the questions raised above: we should deal with the present desolation by clinging to what is old, respected and simple, by imprinting these values on our memories, by carrying them secretly and invisibly until later generations appear that perhaps will be more receptive to them. This is the hope, or the escape, of all conservatives who have to bridge somehow the gap between their cult of the past and the future. In view of the threat posed by the empty present:

> Each slow turn of the world carries such disinherited ones to whom neither the past nor the future belongs.[83]

Rilke feels strengthened in his resolve:

> This shouldn't confuse *us*; no, it should commit us to preserve the form we still can recognize.[84]

A few years later, Hugo von Hofmannsthal will say in *his* poetic last will and testament: "Give testimony that I was there even if no one knew me."[85] But what is it that is supposed to be preserved in this way, in memory, longing and faithfulness of heart? The *thing*—a term so important to Rilke—that consists of equal parts of nature and art, and the simple life, where man and environment, human labor and labor of the earth, had not yet been separated. The *Lettres Milanaises* speak of the "living and loved thing that left the hand of the worker or artisan full of vibrations and that was humanized by usage."[86] The "Ninth Elegy" speaks of the things, the remembering and then pronouncing of which constitutes the profoundest meaning of life and which will awaken admiration even in the unreachable

LYRIC POETRY AND POLITICS

angel:

> Tell him about things. He'll stand amazed, just as you did
> beside the ropemaker in Rome or the potter on the Nile.
> . . . And these things, whose lives
> are lived in leaving—they understand when you praise them.
> Perishing, they turn to us, the most perishable, for help.
> They want us to change them completely in our invisible
> hearts,
> oh—forever—into us!⁸⁷

The Rilke of the *Lettres Milanaises* would like to return to the "rural and village humility"⁸⁸ of earlier times. He hopes, as many of his contemporaries hoped, that Mussolini can lead him back there, Mussolini, in whose country "the gesture, the action, the *visible* example"⁸⁹ had reawakened. Behind all the complaints in the *Lettres Milanaises* there stands the hope that fascism will repair everything again and restore the preindustrial world. In the year the *Elegies* were composed, Rilke had not yet taken such careful notice of fascism but his aspirations nevertheless tended in the same direction, toward a return to the simple life. The dictate of wisdom, the justification of this so very beleaguered and precarious life, consists in showing the world to the otherwise unaffected angel in a condition that for the poet was quite apparently the highest of all: "Show him some simple thing,"⁹⁰ the "Ninth Elegy" says. And the enumeration of "house, bridge, well, gate, jug, olive tree, window . . ." with the characteristic addendum "*at most*, pillar, tower . . ."⁹¹ evokes a bucolic landscape, a patriarchal world of creation and use in which man was not yet alienated from things. This much admired catalogue, however sublime and worthy of respect it might be, in the final analysis glorifies the retreat into the precapitalist past and points forward to the ideology of "blood and earth." To the degree it is to be thought of as a program for the future—

and this we can say today with the shudder of recent memory—it is not at all lacking in certain terrifying, atavistic components.[92]

The psychological and sociological background of this attitude toward *things* has long since been taken account of by social scientists. Descriptions by sociologists characterizing the modern mode of production and the human situation that corresponds to it can be applied in a very precise way to a lyric work like the *Elegies*:

> Man has built his world; he has built factories and houses, he produces cars and clothes, he grows grain and fruit. But he has become estranged from the product of his own hands, he is not really the master any more of the world he has built; on the contrary, this man-made world has become his master, before whom he bows down, whom he tries to placate or manipulate as best he can. The work of his own hands has become his God. He seems to be driven by self-interest, but in reality his total self with all its concrete potentialities has become an instrument for the purposes of the very machine his hands have built. He keeps up the illusion of being the center of the world, and yet he is pervaded by an intense sense of insignificance and powerlessness which his ancestors once consciously felt toward God.[93]

And in reference to Rilke himself, another writer has said: "The aesthetic weakness of this thing cult, the secretive gesture, the amalgamation of religion and craftsmanship, betrays at the same time the real power of reification which can no longer be guilded by any lyrical aura or recovered for the realm of the meaningful."[94]

All this can be productively related to the *Lettres Milanaises* and to the *Duino Elegies* in such a way as to indicate their position within the intellectual climate of our epoch. The conflicts that are worked out in these writings can be subsumed without difficulty under the broad conceptual opposition, culture vs. civilization, which has played an especially important role in the traditional thought of Central Europe. This distinction made it possible for Rilke, like thousands of others, to reject as civilization the disquieting or repulsive elements of the life surrounding him and to hold up as culture that which suited him. "A Culture, to recall Oswald Spengler's words, has a soul, whereas Civilization is 'the most external and artificial state of which humanity is capable.' The acceptance of Culture and the rejection of Civilization meant for many people an end to alienation from their society."[95]

By tracing out these parallels, have we fallen into a "crude sociologism" or have we contributed to the understanding of Rilke and his later lyric poetry? A similar question is raised by Theodor Adorno, a critic experienced in these interrelationships:

"Can anyone but a stranger to the arts speak about lyric poetry and society?" And since he is only speaking *pro domo* and attempting to justify his own critical practice, he provides himself with the following methodological directives: "Apparently the suspicion is only put aside when lyrical constructs are not used as demonstrative illustrations of some set of sociological theses, but rather when their relationship to the social discloses something essential about them, something at the basis of their quality. It should not lead away from the artwork, but more deeply into it."[96]

We feel that we have satisfied this demand. In my view, an awareness of what position the *Duino Elegies* occupy on the intellectual map of the twentieth century is an indispensable prerequisite of a deeper understanding of the texts themselves.

Chapter 6
Conclusion

Contempt for daily politics has a long tradition among German intellectuals.[1] It has long since become clear, however, that in Rilke's case this arrogantly proclaimed distance vis-à-vis politics and history was entirely compatible with an occasional, even passionate, involvement in the ideological disputes and prejudices of his contemporaries. Indeed, we have seen that apolitical credo and political attitude combine in Rilke to constitute a recognizable and characteristic ideological structure, namely, that of the European Right. It turned out that Rilke, like every other human being caught in his own contradictions, was not always oriented in the same direction, but rather that he often vacillated, and in some periods reacted more "liberally," in others more "conservatively." Basically Rilke's stance, as determined both by his origins and by the social identity he himself freely chose, was "old conservative" and "counterrevolutionary." But due to the pressure of historical developments and the influence of particular individuals his ideological stance became increasingly rigid. It can be said that this urbane, sensitive, and in many ways appealing poet, like almost the entire conservative movement of his age, slipped ever more toward the radical rightist side and finally

CONCLUSION

associated himself with a movement that "rejected everything for which free men stand,"[2] and that made use of "a reactionary elite" in order to "perpetuate an obsolete social order under the pretext of defending society—which meant the status quo...."[3]

We can therefore agree with Rilke's biographer when he says the poet was actually not as apolitical as appeared. But we cannot leave his claims unchallenged when, even going so far as to ascribe to Rilke a certain political acumen, he continues: "When he applied his critical intelligence, enlightened by an intuitive clearsightedness, to political matters, his views were more penetrating and often sounder than those of the politically minded newspaper reader and the 'well-informed man.'"[4] If that is true, then it speaks solely against the well-informed contemporaries, not however for Rilke. For Rilke's comprehension of social mechanisms was primitive, his political aspirations were naïve and not at all oriented toward actually existing conditions, his explanations either adhered to mere externalities or missed the point, his observations were superficial, his judgment uncertain and easily misled. Rilke's greatest error in the age of mass movements and collective problems was his extreme individualism, which prevented him from recognizing the real moving forces of his time. For him, a nation reacts like an individual; he applies lessons drawn from the practice of an individual artist to complex structures like the state; the Jewish question is to be solved as if it were a matter of a single individual's difficulties; the poor do not constitute a unified group whose condition derives from common causes, but rather each has his own peculiar misery in his own particular way. For this reason, Rilke remained blind to the enormous powers of his time which compelled and overpowered the individual. In short, he had little sense of history and did not really understand what was actually happening in the world around him. His strength lay in the psychological sphere. He sensed intuitively what psychological correlates were produced in people by social circumstances. With a rhetorical élan that sweeps the reader along, and with a truly splendid stock of images, Rilke lamented what tormented him so about the modern condition while he sang the praise of what he considered inviolate and eternal. In so doing, he enriched that valuable store of truths from which we live. For this reason, we can, as he himself did, evoke the "god of completeness" and declare: we wouldn't want to do without him.

Thus we have arrived at Rilke's poetry. "A writer's political and religious beliefs are not excrescences to be laughed away, but something that will leave their mark even on the smallest detail of his work."[5] These words of George Orwell's register an insight that has not always counted as valid but that is now increasingly establishing itself in the study of literature. To demonstrate that Rilke's vague sociohistorical tendencies influenced every detail of his poetic work was not our intention, nor could it have been. But to show that these tendencies left ineradicable traces on the general orientation of his work, that they helped form it in its entirety—that has been an important and legitimate goal of our investigation. It was not only a matter of trying to find out as accurately as possible what Rilke believed and how he arrived at these beliefs. Our aim was also to make clear how these beliefs and attitudes are reflected in his works, to demonstrate that from the harmless stories of his youth to the seemingly innocent praise of things in his late works there exist very significant interconnections between poetic *oeuvre* and historical world.

The method we have used to reach these results has been a combination of internal and external perspectives.[6] For long stretches the poet's own words provided us with material. Letters and other autobiographical documents as well as literary works were interpreted and their meanings organized according to the procedures of intrinsic criticism. The results gained in this way, however, were confronted

CONCLUSION

with a broad spectrum of relevant literature from the social sciences and history, and only then did those characteristic configurations that transcend the individual case emerge into view. Although not otherwise indebted to him, our method, as regards this one point, corresponds to the requirements set by Lucien Goldmann, a well-known French theoretician: "Given the particularly insufficient character of our knowledge of psychology at present, a parallel study must first of all situate itself on the two planes of the immanent analysis of the work and the insertion of the work into the historical and sociological structures of which it is a part."[7]

It is undeniable that we have only made a start with all this, merely indicated a direction. Repeated mention was made in the course of our study of Rilke's theological and poetological ideas and their connection with his social and political views. More detailed investigations of these interconnections are needed. Other questions arise: How did Rilke support himself? What proportion of his income was constituted by honoraria, by donations from his publisher, by gifts and invitations? How much did his way of life actually cost? Did the relationship among these various factors shift during the course of his life? What was the political orientation of his friends and most important benefactors? With which did he most agree? In other words, can economic or class interests be unequivocally determined in Rilke's case? Are there instances of direct influence in the formation of his political views? The example of Gonzague de Reynolds would fall under this catagory but it could be supplemented by an investigation of certain other French connections of Rilke's. And who are the "beautiful and noble fellows" of Paris and Venice to whom Rilke refers in the *Lettres Milanaises*?[8] The same problematics could also be clarified by studies of reception that would show which ideological and sociological aspects played a role in Rilke's fame. Of course, here too, the literary-theoretical prerequisites have only been meagerly fulfilled. Nothing is more difficult to determine than by whom and for what reasons a writer is honored and praised, his works bought and read. An approach to this entire complex of issues could be opened up by an investigation that undertook to study how Rilke was received by literary critics and in academic research.

For the moment we must be satisfied with the results obtained in the course of this brief inquiry. The reader interested in history can learn from these results how a creative and refined individual reacted in detail to the currents and trends of his age, the forty years from 1885 to 1925. Indeed, sociology is mainly concerned with an anonymity that can be statistically grasped, and the writing of history seldom deals with individuals who lived as distant from the actual historical events as Rilke did. However, the reader who is used to concentrating his attention on poetry and excluding any broader perspective will have to concede that political and social conditions exerted a powerful determining influence on the work of even such a metaphysical and emphatically "apolitical" poet. Mountains and valleys, rivers and meadows, sea and stars are all elements of our earthly habitat. Just like our "inner" nature, the afflictions and the flights of the soul, the effect of love, loneliness, and death, they are essential components of our experience and legitimate themes for the poet. Whose vocation might it be, if not the poet's, to know and to speak of these things?! What Rilke sought was likewise this "most universal, this ultimately valid, this most fundamental aspect of life, the drive for its basic colors and finally once again the drive for the infinite light in which they all, inexhaustibly, surrender themselves."[9] Who would want to think ill of him for doing so? To find a meaning for life that would lie outside all the limitations of time and social circumstance is an ancient and probably inextinguishable dream of mankind. But whoever in his yearning neglects

CONCLUSION

that through which alone life becomes concrete and palpable, namely the historical, whoever would wish to transcend the social and political spheres altogether—that person runs the risk of becoming the advocate of an inhuman barbarism no matter how pure his intentions might be.[10]

What Rilke's example teaches both the student of history and the student of poetry is at least this: a view of life and history that excludes all protest against inhumanity paves the way for domination by the most nefarious of interests. If the times affect us in such a way that we feel we should protest, then we should at least insist upon a social organization or—to put it altogether modestly and realistically—we should declare ourselves for a social order in which that protest need not be suppressed.

Notes

Chapter 1
The Problem

1 For example, Werner Günther, *Weltinnenraum. Die Dichtung Rainer Maria Rilkes* (Bern-Leipzig: Paul Haupt, 1943); Beda Allemann, *Zeit und Figur beim späten Rilke* (Pfüllingen: Neske, 1961).

2 *Lettres Milanaises*, ed., Renée Lang (Paris: Plon, 1956), p. 84.

3 Cf. for example, George L. Mosse, *The Crisis of German Ideology: Intellectual Origins of the Third Reich* (New York: Grosset & Dunlop, 1964), p. 2, on a similar problem: "Much of this ideology has been characterized as 'apolitical,' and indeed at first glance it is hard to see how one can justify calling nature mysticism, sun worship, and theosophy parts of a political ideology. But the problem here is one of perspective. For the ideologists who will be our chief concern, traditional politics was seen as exemplifying the worst aspect of the world in which they lived. They rejected political parties as artificial, and representative government was swept aside in favor of an elitism which derived from their semi-mystical concepts of nature and man. This type of thinking is only apolitical if 'politics' is restricted to a description of traditional forms of activity and belief. If 'politics' is so defined, then the ideology with which we are concerned is more properly termed *anti-political* . . . . Ironically enough, an ideological movement which has been termed 'apolitical' eventually came to define what was politically acceptable."

4 Helmut Kreuzer, *Die Boheme. Beiträge zu ihrer*

NOTES

Beschreibung (Stuttgart: J. B. Metzlersche Verlagsbuchhandlung, 1968), p. 279.

5 *Lettres Milanaises*, p. 97. See Chapter 4, note 115.

6 The assassination of Matteotti, Italian Socialist leader, took place in June, 1924; Rilke's letter was written on February 14, 1926.

Chapter 2
Early Impressions

1 Above all by Peter Demetz in "The Czech Themes of Rainer Maria Rilke," *German Life and Letters* VI (1952–53): 35–49.

2 Peter Demetz writes: "The Rilke family was no exception to this philistine nationalism of the hard-pressed and sterile German upper classes. If anything, it was accentuated by the social failure of Joseph Rilke and the disappointed ambitions of the real mistress of the household, his wife Sophie." Ibid., 35. We can regard the fact that Rilke was not allowed to attend Czech language classes at his high school as a symptom of this aversion.

3 Oskar Wiener, *Deutsche Dichter aus Prag* (Vienna-Leipzig: 1919), p. 8. Quoted here after Peter Demetz, *René Rilkes Prager Jahre* (Düsseldorf: Eugen Diederichs, 1953), p. 141.

4 Especially in the novella "The Family Celebration" ("Das Familienfest") which originated between 1893 and 1895. Cf. Rainer Maria Rilke, *Sämtliche Werke*, herausgegeben vom Rilke-Archiv in Verbindung mit Ruth Sieber-Rilke, besorgt durch Ernst Zinn, 6 vols. (Frankfurt am Main: Insel Verlag, 1955–1965) IV, 9–19. All quotations from Rilke's works, unless otherwise indicated, are taken from this edition. Roman numerals refer to the volume, Arabic numerals to the page.

5 Written in 1898; cf. IV, 512–567.

6 "... downright whipped into growing up by his old embittered father, who couldn't wait for his son to start earning money. Finally he tore him away from his studies just when the boy had found some enjoyment in science, and he considered his duty fulfilled from the moment Ernst was situated and provided for in the pharmacy. . . . 'Now the world stands open to you,' the older Land used . . . to declare. But the young man seemed to have no longing for this 'open world.'" IV, 208–209.

7 IV, 209.

8 Cf. "King Bohusch" ("König Bohusch"), IV, 150–152.

9 IV, 181.

10 IV, 177–178. As if the "burden of poverty" or "misery" had nothing to do with "oppression"! Such statements reveal how poorly informed Rilke was, how far from understanding the mechanisms through which large sections of the population are exploited. These mechanisms are a matter of common knowledge to every student who has taken a few courses in the social sciences. We have no proof at all that Rilke acquired more perspicacious views later in life.

11 IV, 158. The subsequent passage on Rosalka is from IV, 163. The reference to the "Krummauer Castle" is at IV, 162.

12 IV, 220. The reversal from political agitation to imaginative inwardness is a frequent one in the early works. Cf., for example, the story "The Last Ones" ("Die Letzten") from 1901.

13 From *Offering to the Lares (Larenopfer)* I, 45–46.

14 Rilke also remained true to these views years later when the Czechs actually gained national independence and he reaffirmed them in a letter to Czechoslovakia's first president Thomas G. Masaryk, about whom he speaks in tones of the highest respect. See Chapter 4, note 106.

NOTES

15 IV, 134.

16 The cripple is such a frequent representative of the poet that one can speak of a topos.

17 Cf. Demetz, "The Czech Themes of Rainer Maria Rilke," 47.

18 They were written in 1899, published in 1900.

19 Ewald, of course, is right about this. Indeed, one could even include works of Rilke's other than the *Stories of our Dear Lord (Geschichten vom lieben Gott)* in this characterization. The fact that the first-person narrator can be identified, simply and without qualification, with Rilke is demonstrated by a fictive letter from Ewald to Rilke, composed in 1906. Cf. IV, 938–943.

20 These opening sentences of "The Song of Justice" ("Das Lied von der Gerechtigkeit") are at IV, 329.

21 IV, 329 (my italics).

22 Paris, 1876 (Reprint: The Hague, 1967). Both passages at p. 474.

23 IV, 341. The following passage is from IV, 343.

24 IV, 302–308.

25 From the section "On Poverty and On Death" ("Von der Armut und vom Tode") in *The Book of Hours (Das Stundenbuch)* I, 356.

26 IV, 384.

27 Demetz, "The Czech Themes of Rainer Maria Rilke," 43, 48.

28 IV, 982.

29 To Ilse Erdmann, September 11, 1915, in *Briefe*, vol. II, 1914–1926 (Wiesbaden: Insel, 1950), 44.

30 To Rudolf Bodländer, March 13, 1922, in *Briefe aus Muzot,* (Leipzig: Insel Verlag, 1935), 114–115.

31 IV, 98.

Chapter 3
World War

1 For instance, Else Buddeberg, *Rainer Maria Rilke. Eine innere Biographie* (Stuttgart: J.B. Metzlersche Verlagsbuchhandlung, 1955), 31–51.

2 *Florenzer Tagebuch*, in *Tagebücher aus der Frühzeit*, Ruth Sieber-Rilke and Carl Sieber, eds. (Leipzig: Insel, 1942), 36. On the same page we read: "Know then that the artist creates for himself—solely for himself."

3 Ulrich Fülleborn, *Das Strukturproblem der späten Lyrik Rilkes* (Heidelberg: Carl Winter, 1960), 303ff.

4 *Florenzer Tagebuch*, 121.

5 Ibid., 50.

6 Ibid., 52.

7 Ibid., 49.

8 Ibid., 54.

9 Ibid., 48.

10 Ibid., 59–60.

11 For instance, Thorkild Bjornvig, "Die Bedeutung des Weltkrieges für Rilke und sein Werk," *Orbis Litterarum* XI (1956), 13–17.

12 Cf. Chapter 2, note 29.

13 II, 87–92.

14 *Gesammelte Werke 8* (Wiesbaden: Limes, 1968), "Doppelleben," 1947.

15 II, 90.

16 II, 89.

17 II, 91.

18 II, 92.

19 To Anna Freifrau von Münchhausen, August 29, 1914, in *Briefe*, vol. II, 1914–1926 (Leipzig: Insel, 1950), 7.

20 To Karl and Elisabeth von der Heydt, November 6, 1914, in *Briefe*, vol. II, 1914–1926, 15. In a letter to Thankmar Freiherrn von Münchhausen (11) he also explicitly retracts the war poems.

21 In *Rainer Maria Rilke-Inga Junghanns: Briefwechsel* (Wiesbaden: Insel, 1959), 64. The letter is from August 12, 1917.

22 To Ellen Delp, October 10, 1915, *Briefe*, vol. II, 1914–1926, 49.

23 To Thankmar von Münchhausen, June 28, 1915, *Briefe*, vol. II, 1914–1926, 24.

24 To Lou Andreas-Salomé, September 9, 1914, in *Briefe*, vol. II, 1914–1926, 9. He also uses very severe expressions in his correspondence with Marianne Gilbert. Cf. Marianne Gilbert, *Le Tiroir Entr'Ouvert*, précedé d'une introduction de Marcel Brion avec trente et une lettres inédites de R.-M. Rilke traduites par Balise Briod et huit dessins de l'auteur (Paris: Bernard Grasset, 1956). For example: "the insanity of the war" (28); "I have the impression that the entire world has come unhinged, dislocated everywhere, and the more days pass and the less I understand how something so criminal can prolong itself. . . ." (34).

25 Bernhard Blume, "Ding und Ich in Rilke's 'Neuen Gedichten,'" *Modern Language Notes* LXVII (1952), 220.

26 To Count Dietrichstein, June 15, 1917, *Mesa* (Spring, 1952), 27.

27 To Countess Aline Dietrichstein, June 20, 1917, in *Briefe*, vol. II, 1914–1926, 77.

28 To Frl. A. Baumgarten, August 22, 1915, ibid., 34.

29 To Kurt Wolff, March 28, 1917, *The Yale University Library Gazette* XXIV, 3 (January, 1950), 118–128.

30 To Frl. A. Baumgarten, *Briefe*, vol. II, 1914–1926, 34 (my emphasis).

31 To Countess Mary Gneisenau, August 9, 1917, ibid., 83–84.

32 *Junghanns-Briefwechsel*, 64 (see note 21 above).

33 To Thankmar von Münchhausen, in *Briefe*, vol. II, 1914–1926, 24.

34 Ibid.

35 Cf. *Florenzer Tagebuch*, 36: "In this way it comes

to seem as if there were really a relationship of mutuality between the creative individual and the crowd; and many don't even hesitate to jabber on about an educational influence of art on the one hand and about impulses which the artist receives from the people on the other."

36 To Ellen Delp, October 10, 1915, in *Briefe*, vol. II, 1914–1926, 49.

37 Ibid.

38 Cf., for instance, IV, 326–327.

39 To Ellen Delp, October 10, 1915, in *Briefe*, vol. II, 1914–1926, 49.

40 To Clara Rilke, November 7, 1918, in *Briefe*, vol. II, 1914–1926, 110–111.

41 Ibid.

42 Kurt Eisner, socialist leader of the Munich revolution of 1918. Ibid.

43 To Eva Maria Freifrau Heyl zu Herrnstein, March 1, 1919, ibid., 131–132. This letter, by the way, exhibits an equal tolerance in all directions. The same passage contains the following remark: "And on the other hand it must not lead us astray that those who do not yet wish to muster up belief in the maturity of this crowd attempt to secure their position with all the outmoded means of resistance." It would be interesting to determine what the political positions of Rilke's correspondents were in order to see to what degree he accommodated himself to their views.

44 To Dorothea Freifrau von Ledebur, December 19, 1918, in *Briefe 1914–1921*, Ruth Sieber-Rilke and Carl Sieber, eds. (Leipzig: Insel, 1937), 214.

45 To Anni Mewes, December 9, 1918, *Briefe*, vol. II, 1914–1926, 113.

46 Ibid., but also in the letter to Freifrau von Ledebur (see note 44 above).

47 To Anni Mewes, December 9, 1918, in *Briefe*, vol. II, 1914–1926, 113.

48 To Dorothea Freifrau von Ledebur, December 19, 1918, in *Briefe 1914–1921*, 214.

49 Ibid.

50 To Lisa Heise, in *Briefe*, vol. II, 1914–1926, 386.

51 It is striking, for example, that the German contributors to the *Schaubühne* (later *Weltbühne*) underwent similar changes. Carl Schorske ("Weimar and the Intellectuals I," *The New York Review of Books*, May 7, 1970, 24) summarizes this as follows: "Like many other intellectuals, its contributors hailed the war as the great regenerator of a sick society, the creator of a new community. But disillusionment came early, as soon as the prewar social antagonism reemerged. The change of the *Weltbühne* group from cultural to political criticism was completed in a second euphoric experience—that of revolution in November, 1918. Revolution promised the new humane institutions that war had failed to bring."

52 To Anni Mewes, December 9, 1918, in *Briefe*, vol. II, 1914–1926, 113.

53 To Countess Mary Gneisenau, August 9, 1917, in *Briefe*, vol. II, 1914–1926, 84.

Chapter 4
Period of Maturity

1 Cf. Talcott Parsons, "Some Sociological Aspects of the Fascist Movement (1942)," in *Essays in Sociological Theory*, (Glencoe, Ill.: Open Court, 1954), pp 124–141, esp. p. 124. This essay, which we follow in several respects, will hereafter be referred to as "Parsons."

2 To be sure, these factors are not sufficient. Indeed, they had been the dominating phenomena of European developments for a long time while the fascist movements arose in the twentieth century and only attained power after the First World War. Wolfgang Sauer ("National Socialism: Totalitarianism or Fascism," *American Historical Review* LXXIII (1967): 404–424, hereafter referred to as "Sauer")

emphasizes that other preconditions must be fulfilled and speaks of "the importance of the military element for the analysis of fascism." (420) He also argues that it was only with the First World War that the necessary conditions for the development of fascism were established. (411) Others maintain that fascism presupposes crises of liberal democracy. Sauer argues that this is above all true for "fascist attitudes and movements" (421), which, of course, are the focus of our interest here.

3 Sauer, 420.

4 Parsons, 127.

5 I am aware of the enormous complexity which, in the more recent developments, has made concepts like Left and Right nearly meaningless. This, in any case, is the opinion of Eugen Weber (*The European Right, A Historical Profile*, Hans Rogger and Eugen Weber, eds. [Berkeley, Los Angeles: University of California Press, 1965], "Introduction," 2): "It would seem in effect, that the label is cracking. We continue to use it but no longer know, cannot possibly know for sure, quite what it covers, quite what we mean." And: "The more we have inspected the image of the Right, the less sure we have become of what it is." (5) The distinctions we draw in this section, therefore, are to be taken as working definitions in the sense of E. Weber's statement: "Since we cannot analyze Right and Left away, it seems worthwhile to try to understand them." (3)

6 Herman Lebovics, *Social Conservation and the Middle Classes in Germany* (Princeton: Princeton University Press, 1969), pp. 5–6.

7 Sauer, 410–411.

8 The following event reported by Wilhelm Hausenstein (*Rainer Maria Rilke. Stimmen der Freunde. Ein Gedächtnisbuch,* ed. Gert Buchheit [Freiburg i.B.: Urban-Verlag, 1931], 90) can serve as a symbol of this "turn to the left": " . . .I saw how the terrifying outbreak of a white terror in May of the year 1919 destroyed him. The so-called

council period in Munich was past. Whoever was suspect was persecuted with rifle butts. Rifle butt and army boots pounded at Rilke's door one morning at five; he was said to be a Bolshevist. This event drove him out of Germany.''

9 Cf. Iring Fetscher, "Faschismus und Nationalsozialismus: Zur Kritik des sowjetmarxistischen Faschismusbegriffs," *Politische Vierteljahresschrift* III (1962): 48–50. "In a first phase—up to the year 1925—the liberal Minister of Finance *Stefani* followed a finance and economic policy that was extremely well-disposed to enterprise. . . . In July, 1925, however, *Stefani* was replaced by Count *Volpi* and economic policy underwent a considerable turn. . . . This turn . . . ran parallel to the transition from the relatively moderate coalition dictatorship under *Mussolini's* direction to a regime that became ever more acutely authoritarian and finally totalitarian." (Hereafter referred to as "Fetscher.")

10 Sauer, 410.

11 Sauer, 414.

12 Weber, *The European Right*, "Introduction," 4.

13 Cf. Fetscher, 47: "Despite the indisputable support of Italian fascism on the part of industrial and high financial circles, the initial help of the conservatives at the court and in the military leadership nevertheless seems to me to have been more decisive for *Mussolini's* victory. . . . After *Mussolini* had affirmed the monarchy in the summer of 1922, the sympathies of the greater part of the generals were securely his, and since he also had allies in the royal house (the queen mother and the Duke of Aosta), his being entrusted with the formation of the government no longer came as a surprise."

14 Cf. Fetscher, 42: "In the age of world civil war the term 'facist' has become a generally used pejorative term with which no one any longer associates any precise meaning. For the communist of today almost the entire noncommunist world consists of varieties of fascism: the 'social

fascism' of the reformist workers' parties, the 'clerical fascism' of the Christian Socialists and the 'military fascism' of the conservatives and nationalists. But conversely too—in the 'Western camp'—it has become common to speak of the 'red fascism' of the communists. . . ."

15   Eudo C. Mason, *Rilke, Europe, and the English-Speaking World* (Cambridge: Cambridge University Press, 1961), p. 179.

16   To Rudolf Bodländer, March 13, 1922, in *Briefe aus Muzot 1921–1926* (Leipzig: Insel, 1935), 114 (my emphasis).

17   To Xaver von Moos, December 30, 1921, ibid., 78.

18   To Lotte Hepner, November 8, 1915, in *Briefe*, vol. II 1914–1926, 52.

19   J.R. von Salis, *Rainer Maria Rilke: The Years in Switzerland*, trans. N.K. Cruickshank (Berkeley, Los Angeles: University of California Press, 1964), 104.

20   Ibid., 105.

21   "And if we speak of loneliness again, then it becomes ever more clear that it is not in essence anything one can choose or not. We *are* lonely. . . . " *Briefe an einen jungen Dichter*, Insel-Bücherei, 406 (Leipzig: Insel, 1950), 46.

22   Cf. Erich Simenauer, *Rainer Maria Rilke* (Bern: Paul Haupt, 1953); Hermann von Jan, *Rilkes Aufzeichnungen des Malte Laurids Brigge* (Leipzig: Weber, 1938).

23   Cf. George Mosse, *The Crisis of German Ideology: Intellectual Origins of the Third Reich* (New York: The Universal Library-Grosset & Dunlop, 1964), 6: "The word 'rootedness' occurs constantly in their vocabulary." Cf. also 15–16, 17, 20, 22, 28ff., 55, 57.

24   Parsons, 125–126.

25   Parsons (125) employs here terminology that was first introduced by Durkheim. Our use of the term *Anomie* follows that of Parsons.

26   Cf. the widely read book by Erich Fromm, *Escape*

from Freedom (New York: Holt, Rinehart and Winston, 1941).

27   Salis (*Rainer Maria Rilke. The Years in Switzerland*, 105) also emphasizes the poet's unbourgeois character.

28   *Die Briefe an Frau Gudi Nölke*, ed. Paul Obermüller (Leipzig: Insel, 1953), letter 39 from February 12, 1923. To be sure, like all of us, Rilke requires a special, personal occasion or stimulus in order to attend to such perceptions. The fact that his friend, the ballerina Baladine Klossowska, was living in very unfortunate circumstances in the inflation in Berlin will not have been without influence on Rilke's mood. Even here the connection between knowledge and human interests has an effect.

29   Barrington Moore Jr., *Social Origins of Dictatorship and Democracy* (Boston: Beacon Press, 1966), 485.

30   Fülleborn, *Das Strukturproblem der späten Lyrik Rilkes*, 336.

31   Carl E. Schorske, "Weimar and the Intellectuals II," *The New York Review of Books*, May 21, 1970, pp. 21–22. Let us also note what Schorske has to say about the term "Mittelstand" which we have used, along with many sociologists, instead of his preferred term "bourgeois": "The term means 'middle estate,' implying status in a feudal, hierarchical order. Yet 'Mittelstand,' for all its feudal ring, is not a truly feudal term. It arose in the nineteenth century, and was developed by conservative social theorists to apply to the preindustrial artisans, shopkeepers, peasants, etc. threatened by the new industrial capitalism. The term expressed nostalgia for the lost privileges and rights of medieval guildsmen, and a claim to status independent of wealth. Above all, the concept of 'estate' offered a psychological refuge. . . . "

32   What follows has often been presented but must be repeated, at least in outline, in this context. We continue to follow Parsons, whose essay from the first years of the

war offers a most concise account of the various causes of fascism.

33 This is the thesis of the above quoted article by Iring Fetscher.

34 Sauer, 417. By "lower-class" Sauer means: "peasants," "small businessmen," "white-collar workers," "lower levels of the professions." The "upper-class" groups would be "the aristocracy, the large landlords, the higher bureaucrats, . . ." Ibid.

35 See also note 29 above.

36 Sauer, 417.

37 Ibid.

38 Along with these points (the city, technology, the social question, race, nationalism) the capitalist economic system and its central symbols "money" and "profit" ought to be investigated. Rilke's remarks on these latter factors, however, are too little developed to warrant a section of their own. Nevertheless, several of the passages we refer to will show that he was unequivocally *opposed* to these capitalist key terms.

39 VI, 742.

40 Ibid.

41 VI, 743.

42 "Von der Armut und vom Tode," I, 343–366.

43 This distinction is one of the most important on which the book by Beda Allemann (*Zeit und Figur beim späten Rilke*) is based.

44 I, 345.

45 I, 355.

46 I, 363.

47 I, 345.

48 I, 353–354.

49 For instance, in Antonio de Guevara, *Libro de menosprecio dela corte y alabança dela aldea*, 1539.

50 *Briefe aus Muzot*, 335–336.

51 Mason, *Rilke, Europe, and the English-Speaking World*, 155–156.

NOTES

52   Ibid., 158.
53   II, 246.
54   To Nora Purtscher-Wydenbruck, September 25, 1921, in *Briefe aus Muzot*, 33.
55   Ibid., 35.
56   To Anni Mewes, 1919, in Franz Theodor Csokor, "Der Kornett und die Feldwebel—Aus unbekannten Rilke-Briefen," *Stuttgarter Zeitung*, December 29, 1951.
57   John R. Harrison has studied the Anglo-Saxon side of this development in *The Reactionaries: Yeats, Lewis, Pound, Eliot, Lawrence: A Study of the Anti-Democratic Intelligentsia* (New York: Schocken, 1967).
58   II, 135.
59   Salis, *Rainer Maria Rilke. The Years in Switzerland*, 229. At another point he says more accurately that Rilke's friends were all either artists or aristocrats. Here one ought to mention Marthe, but she is conspicuous as an exception. And in the final analysis she too is absorbed into the artistic world. (105)
60   Hermann Pongs, "Drei unveröffentlichte Briefe Rilkes," *Dichtung und Volkstum, NF des Euphorion* XXXVII (1936), 100–115. Now reprinted in *Briefe aus Muzot*, No. 98 to Professor Hermann Pongs, October 21, 1924, 320–337.
61   Pongs, ibid., 100. Rilke had set the following remark at the head of his journal *Wegwarten*, which carried the subtitle "Songs given to the People" ("Lieder, dem Volke geschenkt"): "Just one word: . . . You offer your works in inexpensive editions. You thereby make it easier for the rich to buy; you do not help the poor. For the poor everything is too expensive. And if it's a matter of two farthings and the question is: book or bread? they'll take the bread; do you blame them? If you want therefore to give to everyone—*then give!*" III, 112. "Wegwarten" is the name of a humble flower.
62   My emphasis; this is the center of Rilke's view of social questions.
63   Here is Rilke's old idea about the inner advantages

of human misery. Given our experiences of the recent past, we can more easily see how absurd it is.

64 Here we can see that Rilke viewed social conditions as natural ones. He therefore did not arrive at the thought that human misery could be produced by human beings, and consequently the simple solution of helping men by ceasing to make them miserable likewise never occurred to him. This would not affect the freedom of the poor, but perhaps that of the rich.

65 The reference here is in all likelihood to "The Song of the Dwarf" ("Das Lied des Zwerges") I, 454–455, and "The Song of the Beggar" ("Das Lied des Bettlers") I, 448–449, both from *The Book of Images (Das Buch der Bilder)*.

66 Whoever believes in the revelatory force of metaphors will be especially intrigued by the expression "varieties." It recalls a zoo, which of course is all the "better" the more varieties of animals are represented there so that one can take "joy" at the abundance offered to view. To be sure, as far as a zoo is concerned, no one would think of "improving" it by eliminating a rare species of bird.

67 A passage like this makes the expression "provided that each was genuinely and entirely peasant girl, maidservant, princess, worker or artist" (Salis, *Rainer Maria Rilke. The Years in Switzerland*, 229) altogether clear in its meaning.

68 Here we find in a somewhat more obscure form the same thought as in *The Stories of our Dear Lord*: poverty is willed by God.

69 Pongs, "Drei unveröffentlichte Briefe," 111f.

70 I assume that the pathos-laden exclamation "We've experienced this" refers to the Russian Revolution.

71 Marianne Gilbert, *Le Tiroir Entr'Ouvert* (See Chapter III, note 32), 26ff. Just the mention of the name Romain Rolland in a positive context illustrates the political change that took place in Rilke's views between the war

and the mid-twenties—or perhaps illustrates what an exceptional interlude the war represented in Rilke's political development. In the *Lettres Milanaises* he explicitly distances himself from the humanitarian views of the same writer: "I am going to astonish you by saying to you that I am infinitely opposed to the poetry . . . which, by its very program, pretends to be especially good and 'humane.' It is precisely that which separates me from a writer like Romain Rolland, whom I esteem very highly without being able to associate myself with his intentions no matter how noble they might be." (84) But during the war Rilke was apparently in agreement with Rolland's "intentions" and with his "cause that is just as good as it is necessary" (from the letter to Marianne Gilbert quoted above).

72 Unpublished letter to Kurt Eisner from January 21, 1918. A photocopy of this letter is in the Munich Stadtbibliothek.

73 It is interesting to note that this language of social concern coincides in Rilke's life and thought with what Ulrich Fülleborn (*Das Strukturproblem der späten Lyrik Rilkes,* 318ff.) calls Rilke's expressionist crisis of the years 1912–1914.

74 *Lettres Milanaises,* 87.

75 To Leonid Pasternak, in *Briefe aus Muzot,* 87.

76 To Herrn von W. [Reinold von Walter], April 6, 1921, reprinted in *Der Gral, Monatsschrift für Dichtung und Leben* XXIII (1929), 399–400.

77 Certain allusions indicate that the letter is addressed to Verhaeren, Rilke's much admired friend who was killed during the war.

78 "Letter of a Young Laborer" ("Der Brief des jungen Arbeiters"), VI, 1121–1122.

79 This comparison is not meant loosely. I am, of course, aware that much speaks against a relationship between Rilke and Protestantism. Erich Fromm sees the beginning of the development of modern totalitarianism in

Luther. Cf. the chapter "Freedom in the Age of the Reformation" in *Escape from Freedom*, esp. 100-101, where the figure of Luther is discussed. The points of contact with Rilke are apparent. Fromm follows, of course, Max Weber's *The Protestant Ethic and the Spirit of Capitalism*, Tawney's *Religion and the Rise of Capitalism*, and Herbert Marcuse's *Authority and Family*. However, he also cites very convincing passages from Luther himself. On the other hand, it has been said of Rilke that he only felt comfortable in Catholic countries and that he reacted strongly against societies with a highly Protestant character, for instance, Northern Germany, England, the United States. An investigation of Rilke's theology, especially its hidden affinities with Protestantism and Catholicism, and above all in its relation to socio-political questions, still needs to be undertaken. Similarly, the efforts to define fascism in relation to the two great branches of Christianity are indecisive.

80 Mosse, *The Crisis of German Ideology*, 7. On the same page he speaks of a "revolution of the soul." Eugen Weber (*The European Right*, 9) remarks: "They were not satisfied with things as they were, but shunned the prospect of proletarian revolution."

81 Cf. the chapter "The Anti-Jewish Revolution" in Mosse, *The Crisis of German Ideology*, 294-311.

82 *Lettres Milanaises*, 96: "I have since childhood envied the great Russian, Jewish and Moslem unities because their national element coincides with a profound religious dictate."

83 Cf. Eduard Goldstücker, "Rilke und Werfel–Zur Geschichte ihrer Beziehungen. Vier bisher unbekannte Briefe Rilkes an Werfel," *Panorama* V, 6 (June, 1961): 21-36.

84 *Rainer Maria Rilke und Marie Thurn und Taxis—Briefwechsel*, besorgt durch Ernst Zinn, 2 vols. (Zürich: Niehaus und Rokytansky, 1951), I, 323. (Hereafter referred to as *Thurn und Taxis--Briefwechsel*.)

NOTES

85 *Ibid.* Letter of February 14, 1914, I, 356.

86 Even Salis (*Rainer Maria Rilke. The Years in Switzerland*, 172) acknowledges: "Rilke was not free from a vague 'blood mysticism'...."

87 *Thurn und Taxis—Briefwechsel*, I, 324, letter of October 21, 1913.

88 The statement is from February 13, 1903, quoted here after Helmut Kreuzer, *Die Boheme*, 246. Kreuzer's commentary provides an extensive account of the development of an aesthetics of creativity and its culmination in the *l'art pour l'art* ideology of the turn of the century.

89 To Jeanne de Sepibus-de-Preux, June 14, 1924, in: Maurice Zermatten, *Les années valaisannes de Rilke* (Sierre: Oskar Amaker, 1951), p. 145.

90 Ilse Blumenthal-Weiss ("Rainer Maria Rilke und das Judentum," *Deutsche Rundschau* LXXXIV (1958), 268–279, esp. 274 and 277) refers to the episodes with Lissauer and Karl Kraus as well as the anti-Semitism of Rilke's mother.

91 May 24, 1924, *Thurn und Taxis—Briefwechsel*, II, 807–808.

92 Ilse Blumenthal-Weiss. "Rainer Maria Rilke und das Judentum."

93 "Rainer Maria Rilke und Arthur Schnitzler: Ihr Briefwechsel mit Anmerkungen," ed. Heinrich Schnitzler, *Wort und Wahrheit* XIII (1958), 283–298. The first quotation is from a letter to Arthur Schnitzler (283), the second from a letter to Rudolf Christoph Jenny which Heinrich Schnitzler reprints in his annotation to page 294. Jenny was the author of the popular play *Need Knows No Commandment (Noth kennt kein Gebot)*.

94 Cf. note 82 above.

95 To Ilse Blumenthal-Weiss, December 28, 1921, in *Briefe aus Muzot*, 64.

96 April 25, 1922, ibid., 130–134. Rilke's emphases are underlined, mine in italics. In the summer of 1903, Rilke

had already expressed his views on the "solution of the Jewish question" ("Lösung der Judenfrage") in his response to a questionnaire circulated by Dr. Julius Moses (VI, 1003–1005). There we find the same ideas but in a less-developed version than in the letters to Ilse Blumenthal-Weiss: the unity of race and religion, the return to the great ancient God. Another statement of Rilke's deserves mention here. In a letter to Frau Wunderly-Volkart from January 16, 1923, he once again employs a double perspective which, however, is rapidly reduced to one-sidedness and finally becomes altogether negative. The Jews, he argues, are on the one hand attractive and even valuable, on the other hand they force one to repel them. This contradiction is resolved in terms of a dialectic of being and appearance: the Jews are indispensable as cultural stimulators, but they are really only the bearers of culture, never its creators. The content of the cultural product is a matter of complete indifference to them; one thing is as good as another. One often gladly receives and appropriates what the Jews offer, but the bearer of this gift is soon felt to be superfluous and even irritating. This is the reason why he, Rilke, has never been able to form a close friendship with a Jew. Cf. Rainer Maria Rilke, *Briefe an Nanny Wunderly-Volkart*, Im Auftrag der Schweizerischen Landesbibliothek und unter Mitarbeit von Niklaus Bigler besorgt durch Rätus Luck, 2 vols. (Frankfurt a. M.: Insel Verlag, 1977), II, 848–849.

97 Ilse Blumenthal-Weiss, "Rainer Maria Rilke und das Judentum," 276.

98 To Herrn von W., June 4, 1921, in *Der Gral. Monatsschrift für Dichtung und Leben* XXIII (1929), 399–400.

99 Wilhelm Mühlon, *Die Verheerung Europas. Aufzeichnungen aus den ersten Kriegsmonaten* (Zurich, 1918), 67. An English version of this book appeared under the name *The Vandal of Europe* (New York and London: G.P. Putnam's Sons, 1918).

100 Ibid., 73. Another passage from Mühlon's book

NOTES

in which he speaks of the failure of writers and artists remains relevant today and has special bearing on our particular line of investigation: "Unfortunately the best-known poets and writers in our country have proven to be poor leaders and little inclined toward creating a spirit of reconciliation. One must doubt whether it was right to give ourselves over to their feelings and aspirations in such an unrestrained manner as we have often and happily done; one must fear that there lay hidden in their works a danger that we innocently never noticed. Their statements during this war have shown us that they do not possess the intellectual superiority that we now require. This recognition must help us after the war to move beyond the celebrities of the recent past. A new generation must seek new poets and leaders who are better beings than those angels with hearts of the devil." Ibid., 141-142.

    101   Salis (*Rainer Maria Rilke. The Years in Switzerland*, 48-49) quotes important passages from Rilke's correspondence with Mühlon in which his agreement with the author's views is clearly expressed.

    102   *Briefe an eine junge Frau*, Insel-Bücherei, 409 (Leipzig: Insel, 1950), 43.

    103   *Rainer Maria Rilke—Briefwechsel mit Benvenuta* (Esslingen: Bechtl, 1954), letter of February 14, 1914.

    104   To Witold von Hulewics, February 15, 1924, in *Briefe aus Muzot*, 236.

    105   From an unpublished letter to Anton Kippenberg from March 26, 1925. The letter is preserved in the Deutsches Literaturarchiv, Schiller-Nationalmuseum, Marbach a.N..

    106   Quoted by Salis (*Rainer Maria Rilke. The Years in Switzerland*, 171-172).

    107   Ibid.

    108   *Die literarische Welt* III, Nr. 2 (1927), 3. The first quotation is from an essay by Eduard Korrodi entitled "The French Rilke" ("Der französische Rilke"), the second from

the facsimile of a letter from Rilke to Mehring. Cf. Walter Mehring, "Der Fall Rilke," *Das Tagebuch* VI (1925): 1214–1215. Cf. also the letter to Dr. Eduard Korrodi from March 20, 1926, *Briefe aus Muzot*, 374–380.

109   *Lettres Milanaises*, 94.
110   Ibid., 95. The emphasis of "abuse" is Rilke's, the emphasis of "German" mine.
111   Ibid., 77.
112   "My dear Rilke, I am not an admirer of Mussolini. I understand perfectly that certain of his speeches could make a good impression. . . . One cannot deny him other merits as well. It would take too long to tell you all the reasons which, since the beginning, have made any adherence to fascism on my part impossible. I would only say to you that for my part I detest violence and I support it even less when it acts in my favor or on behalf of my social class than when it is adopted by my enemies. In the second place, I think that domestic tranquility is assured only when liberty permits one to have an exact idea of what the country thinks and wants—at least a minimum of liberty, which is, besides, the first right acquired by civilization." Ibid., 78. What an admirable woman! "She has his test and he didn't pass," one is tempted to say, with Malte where he speaks of Goethe's correspondence with Bettina. "Perhaps someday it will be shown that here lay the limit of his greatness." VI, 898. These words of Rilke's acquire a special relevance in view of his own correspondence with a young Italian woman who reacted to the fascist monstrosity so much more spontaneously, humanely, and correctly than the great poet.
113   Rilke will have read the speech in *Popolo d'Italia* (No. 1, January 1, 1926) or in French translation. It is reprinted in *Opera Omnia di Benito Mussolini*, vol. 22 (Firenze, 1957), pp. 47–49.
114   Rilke met the Rome enthusiast Alfred Schuler

during the war, heard his lectures, and thought very highly of him. See Chapter 5, note 8.

115 Peter Demetz writes: "Rilke's admiration for Monsieur Mussolini owes more to the spirit of the times than it seems. During the twenties a good deal from the ideology of the French and Italian Right (the emphasis on Latinity, the demand for social order, a pronounced distrust of the post-war democracies) can also be found in the essays of Ezra Pound and T.S. Eliot. "Epochen der Rilke-Deutung," *Merkur* II (1957): 985–991.

116 Fetscher asserts that Mussolini " . . . proclaimed at the beginning full of pride that Italian fascism had *no* ideology at all. . . . In place of this missing ideology there stood a certain theatrical style: heroic stance, fascist greeting, battle calls. . . . " (60) And: "The conservatives, however, did not sympathize with his plebeian methods, but they did sympathize with his nationalistic slogans." (47) This seems to have been the case with Rilke as well.

117 *Lettres Milanaises*, 97. Madame Gallarati-Scotti, of course, had already said—quite rationally—that a modicum of freedom is necessary in order to know what a people thinks and wants.

118 *Lettres Milanaises* 96–97.

119 III, 15–16.

120 And this only a few years after the fiasco of his own military service, about which he writes in an unpublished letter to the wife of the publisher S. Fischer (February 23, 1917, preserved in the Deutsches Literaturarchiv, Schiller-Nationalmuseum, Marbach a.N.) that even as much as twenty-five years later a repetition of the limbo of his military service would have seemed to him the greatest of horrors because it would have reawakened all the old resistances and reversed the process of coming to terms with the experience altogether.

121 *Lettres Milanaises*, 93–94.

122   Ibid., 94.
123   Ibid., 98.
124   Ibid., 95. Demetz ("Epochen der Rilke-Deutung") is of course right to speak of the "kleindeutsch" perspective when Rilke opines that all this has been destroyed "beneath the bondage to a preponderant and arrogant Prussia."
125   Barrington Moore (*Social Origins of Dictatorship and Democracy*, p. 451) associates fascism with the elder Cato and calls the entire phenomenon *Catonism*: "The phenomenon is not confined to modern times nor to Western civilization. The key elements in the rhetoric—advocacy of the sterner virtues, militarism, contempt for 'decadent' foreigners, and anti-intellectualism—appear in the West at least as early as Cato the Elder (234–149 B.C.) who operated his own *latifundium* with slave labor." I assume that this comparison places Moore in the company of those historians who see in fascism a reedition of classical forms of tyranny and oriental despotism. Cf. Sauer, 406: "In addition, a fourth interpretation that has emerged since the war defines Nazism as but a modern variant of classical tyranny. Held mainly by British historians, this view rejects the thesis . . . that totalitarian dictatorship is an entirely new phenomenon." Whatever the case may be, it is entirely worthwhile to read what Barrington Moore has to say about Catonism (491–496).
126   Cf. Mosse, *The Crisis of German Ideology*, 54. See also the use Hugo von Hofmannsthal makes of the symbol Dürer in his "Briefe eines Zurückgekehrten," *Prosa II* (Frankfurt a.M.: S. Fischer, 1959), 293–294.
127   *Briefe an eine junge Frau*, 44–45. A letter to Frau Wunderly-Volkart from January 16, 1923 is especially revealing in this context because it addresses itself to concrete questions of politics, for instance, the occupation of the Ruhr by the French whom Rilke defends for their action. In addition, the letter adds new nuances to Rilke's view of

Germany. Nowhere is his revulsion for the profiteers and the weapons-makers of the postwar era more clearly expressed than here. Especially surprising is Rilke's prophecy that those groups to whom the true health of the nation is a matter of indifference would get along very well with the Soviets if such an alliance suited their particular needs and aims. He speaks of the infamy and the arrogance of the Germans who will yet deliver the entire world over to Bolshevism. We find here the typical perspective of the rightist conservative who regards capitalism and communism as closely related. Rilke always speaks of groups, even of entire peoples, as if they were individuals endowed with a single will. This simplification prevents him from taking notice of the complex dynamics of social life. Cf. *Briefe an Nanny Wunderly-Volkart*, 854–856.

128 "a salutary and certain violence," *Lettres Milanaises*, 85.

129 "so great and impatient is my desire for order," ibid., 88.

130 "Liberty! Isn't it she who makes the world sick?" ibid., 85.

131 "This empty and vain parliamentarianism," ibid.

132 "This hunt for lucre," ibid.

133 Sauer (420) emphasizes "the importance of the military element for the analysis of fascism. . . . Only after total war had militarized European societies and had created large military interests were the conditions required for fascism complete."

134 Rilke himself employs this word: "In the same way, this fury of nationalism is necessary for peoples in order that they touch their own mysterious heart, in order that they feel themselves *one* and united. . . . " *Lettres Milanaises*, 94. This too belongs to the radicalization of the Right. Eugen Weber writes: "The numinous nature of the Nation is something quite different from the mere collection of voters slouching off to the polls: it is *a mystery*." (*The

European Right "Introduction," 24) That sounds like a paraphrase of certain Rilkean statements from the *Lettres Milanaises*. The slogan "one and united" belongs in the same category: "The new slogan . . . was a call for unity, above and beyond parties." (ibid., 9.) Of course, we are only speaking here in general, abstract terms. It is fairly certain that Rilke would have been revolted at the vulgarity of the Nazis. On the other hand, he did not escape the widespread yearning for a "leader," even if that leader be someone who takes us to our destruction: "Who will help? On all sides only those who exploit the dim state of things, nowhere a helper, a leader, a great superior person. To be sure, there may have been such epochs before, full of demise, but were they similarly without form? Without a figure, which would gather everything around itself and extend everything out from itself: *in this way* the tensions and counter-tensions form without a center that would make them into constellations, into orders, at least into orders of demise. . . . " To Leopold von Schlözer, January 21, 1920, in *Briefe*, Vol. II, 1914–1926, 172.

Chapter 5
Lyric Poetry and Politics

1 To be sure, Georg Lukács writes: "It is therefore no accident that the position of the German in the age of Wilhelminian imperialism is most purely expressed by the great lyric poets. They are, one could say, the keys to the decipherment of the epic and dramatic works of this period." *Deutsche Literatur während des Imperialismus* (Berlin: Aufbau Verlag, n.d.), 28. Like us, Lukács notes the "sense of being lost" that is audible in many of Rilke's verses. However, to make Rilke for that reason a lyric poet of Wilhelminian "security" and of "Wilhelminian imperi-

NOTES

alism" is certainly one of those *terrible simplifications* that literary historiography teems with.

2   For instance, Beda Allemann, *Zeit und Figur beim späten Rilke*, pp. 299-300: Critics had "concentrated on the elegies—that is, poetry which, despite its splendid character, nevertheless on the whole represents more of a liquidation of European symbolism in its German variant than the achievement of a new poetic dimension. Connected with this, perhaps, is the fact that research interest has gradually shifted to the Orpheus sonnets, which even Rilke himself at first underestimated as a mere auxiliary product to the elegies. They are the invisible monument that stands at the entrance to the lyric poetry of Rilke's five last years of life. As a characterization of this authentic body of late work, however, the formula of an idyllic rest after 'accomplished work' has presented itself to critics all too easily. The most important poems of this last period . . . can not even be perceived from within this perspective that renders them so harmless." For a similar view, cf. Otto Friedrich Bollnow, "Das Weltbild des reifen Rilke," *Universitas* VII (1952), 681-692.

3   Rainer Maria Rilke, *Duino Elegies and The Sonnets to Orpheus*, trans. A. Poulin, Jr. (Boston: Houghton Mifflin Co., 1977), I, 1. Poulin's translation of both the *Elegies* and the *Sonnets* has been used throughout this chapter except where a particular interpretive point demanded a slightly different translation. (Such cases are indicated as D.W.) The references to this translation will be indicated in the footnotes as "Poulin" along with the poem number (Roman numerals) and the line number(s) (Arabic numerals) for the *Elegies*, part and poem number for the *Sonnets*.

4   The fictional letter "Der Brief des jungen Arbeiters" was written between the fifth and seventh of September, 1921. Cf. above, Ch. 4, Note 78.

5   To Witold von Hulewics, February 13, 1925, *Briefe aus Muzot*, 337.

6 "The 'angel' of the elegies has nothing to do with the angel of the Christian heaven (more perhaps with the angel figures of Islam). . . ." Ibid.

7 Poulin, I, 8–9.

8 I, 685 (D.W.).

9 Jacob Steiner (*Rilkes Duineser Elegien* [Bern und München: Francke, 1962] 21) interprets the word as follows: "Our interpretation of the world is only a cataloguing and labeling. We thereby rigidify the world which, however, is authentically itself only in living relations. We exclude everything that doesn't fit into this determinate interpretation."

10 Poulin, VIII, 66, 68–69.

11 The essay is available in: Alfred Schuler, *Fragmente und Vorträge aus dem Nachlaβ*, mit einer Einführung von Ludwig Klages (Leipzig: Johann Ambrosius Barth, 1940).

12 Cf. the letter of January 18, 1920 to Marie von Thurn und Taxis, *Thurn und Taxis—Briefwechsel*, 585–589.

13 Cf. Marianne Gilbert, *Le Tiroir Entr'Ouvert*, 35; *Thurn und Taxis—Briefwechsel*, I, 409; and the letter to Schuler himself, *Briefe 1914–1921*, 171.

14 To Marie von Thurn und Taxis, March 18, 1915, *Thurn und Taxis—Briefwechsel*, I, 408–411.

15 To Clara Rilke, April 23, 1923, *Briefe aus Muzot*, 207–208.

16 Schuler, *Fragmente und Vorträge*, 192–197.

17 Helmut Kreuzer, *Die Boheme*, 243. I might mention that Ludwig Klages's introduction to the *Fragmente und Vorträge* of Schuler is full of anti-Semitic slurs of the most irrational sort. The texts by Schuler, however, despite several mentions of the Jews, are free of such perfidy.

18 Weber, "Introduction," 24.

19 Poulin, First Series, Sonnet 14.

20 Rudolf Krämer-Badoni, "Rilke und Bachofen," *Berliner Hefte* III (1949), 156.

21   Cf. Poulin, VII, 84–85: "oh, even a lover, alone at the window at night . . ./doesn't she reach your knee?"
22   I, 685 (D.W.).
23   I, 689 (D.W.).
24   I, 723 (D.W.).
25   I, 711 (D.W.).
26   Poulin, IX, 44–46.
27   Rudolf Kassner, *Buch der Erinnerung* (Leipzig: Insel, 1938), 318. The same author writes elsewhere that Rilke "had no feeling for history, for its pragmatic course." "Rainer Marie Rilke. Zum zwanzigsten Todestag," *Umgang der Jahre* (Erlenbach-Zürich: Eugen Rentsch Verlag, 1949), 392.
28   Marie von Thurn und Taxis, *Briefe*, vol. II, 1914–1926, 41.
29   To Adelheid von der Marwitz, January 14, 1919, *Briefe*, vol. II, 1914–1926, 119.
30   For example, in his commentary on the Jewish question. Cf. above, Ch. 4, note 96 and the accompanying quotation.
31   An important exception here is Peter Demetz, "Weltinnenraum und Technologie," *Sprache im technischen Zeitalter XVII–XVIII* (1966): 4–11.
32   Poulin, VII, 52–62. A good paraphrase of this passage with commentary is provided by Eudo C. Mason (*Rilke, Europe and the English-Speaking World*, 165). Jacob Steiner's explication (*Rilkes Duineser Elegien*, 163–164) is even more concise.
33   Jacob Steiner (33) suggests that the *Ge-* prefix of "Gebild" ("structure" in Poulin's translation) has a pejorative connotation. This probably results more from the missing *-e*: "Gebilde" would not have the same effect.
34   When Salis (*Rainer Maria Rilke: The Years in Switzerland*, 124) calls Rilke a "lover of the eighteenth century," it at best applies to the art of the period and to the *ancien régime*. Whether a "château in rococo style" (ibid.)

such as Rilke first dreamed of would have suited him better than the medieval tower of Muzot can remain an open question. We shall soon see that Rilke regarded the entire period from the Middle Ages to the prerevolutionary eighteenth century as an exemplary and unified epoch.

35   Cf. I, 712.

36   The context suggests that "Temples" is to be understood figuratively and can be taken to represent all things "prayed to, served, and knelt to."

37   Poulin, VII, 65–66.

38   I, 718 (D.W.).

39   Cf. Poulin, IX, 50–52.

40   This view is shared by most of the interpreters. Steiner (*Rilkes Duineser Elegien*, 232–233) disputes it.

41   The sonnet "O das Neue, Freunde, ist nicht dies" was originally intended as No. 21 of the first part. See the annotation at II, 759–760.

42   Poulin, First Series, Sonnet 18.

43   Poulin, Second Series, Sonnet 10.

44   Poulin, Second Series, Sonnet 10.

45   Poulin, X, 16 (my emphasis).

46   Poulin, X, 19.

47   Poulin, X, 21.

48   Poulin, X, 23.

49   Poulin, X, 24.

50   I, 722 (D.W.).

51   Poulin, X, 25–27.

52   Poulin, X, 35–36.

53   It is perhaps not superfluous to emphasize once again that I do not at all mean to blame Rilke simply because he shared this disgust with the advocates of the European—and not just the European—Right. What makes his condemnation *politically* significant and susceptible to a critical diagnosis is the cumulative effect, the appearance of a symptom in connection with other symptoms. (Cf. note 54.) The *poetic* effectiveness of the condemnation derives from

NOTES

two sources: first, the superb, detailed comparison between modern city life and a fair, and second, the *truth* of what is being said. Rilke may have viewed matters one-sidedly, but nevertheless the modern city *does* possess horrifying traits.

54 Similar groupings are to be found throughout the literature on fascism. Thus Fetscher (52) points out that resentment against the city, industrialism, and high finance is expressed both in the program of the Nazis and in the ideology of the Hessian People's Confederation ("Hessischer Volksbund") so that regional party members constituted an ideal reservoir of Nazi voters.

55 *Lettres Milanaises*, 85.
56 Ibid., 87.
57 Ibid., 87.
58 Ibid., 85.
59 Ibid., 85.
60 Ibid., 87.
61 Ibid., 84.
62 Poulin, Second Series, Sonnet 9.
63 Poulin, Second Series, Sonnet 11. What Rilke is aiming for here is a rejection of everything that is usually subsumed under the concept of progress: "Soon whoever praised the new will fall silent." II, 135.
64 *Lettres Milanaises*, 86.
65 Ibid., 84–85.
66 Ibid., 85. Rilke probably began to feel a bit queasy at this hymn to violence and brutality since he asks himself a bit later: "Is it because I myself am sick that I recommend the use of a regimen, of a remedy which always calls for authority, a certain temporary violence and a deprivation of freedom?" Ibid., 88. But this slight case of remorse and self-doubt—the only one in this long river of letters ("lettres-fleuve") as the editor calls them—does not last. Immediately the justification of brutality is resumed: "Injustice was always intertwined with all human movements,

it is inherent in them; if one knows a way to the future, one must not lose time avoiding injustice; it is necessary simply to surpass it with action." Ibid. That history is unjust and that its transformations occur not by democratic decision but rather by virtue of violent catastrophes that sweep aside both good and evil, guilty and innocent—this is the doctrine of all rightist fanatics, and among them especially of the poets who have powerful reserves of sensitivity to overcome.

67   *Lettres Milanaises*, 85.

68   "I am going to astonish you by saying that I feel infinitely opposed to consciously 'poetic' poetry which, by virtue of its very program, pretends to be especially goodwilled and 'humane' . . . But I suppose that there [in the political domain], as in poetry, purely humane intentions, voluntarily humane intentions, are not worth a lot. A poetry that would *want* to console or aid or support I don't know what noble conviction would be a sort of weakness which is occasionally touching . . . ; what is decisive is not a charitable or mild intention, but obedience to an authoritarian dictate that *wants* neither good nor evil (about which we know so little). . . . " ibid., 83–84.)

69   John R. Harrison, *The Reactionaries: Yeats, Lewis, Pound, Eliot, Lawrence*, 197.

70   Ibid., 195–196.

71   Weber, "Introduction," 27–28.

72   Poulin, VII, 50.

73   Poulin, VII, 61–62.

74   Poulin, IX, 66–69.

75   One of the few hints in Rilke's writings that the French Revolution destroyed something irrecoverable.

76   Poulin, X, 39–40.

77   *Lettres Milanaises*, 86.

78   Ibid., 86–87. The emphases in the translation-paraphrase are, of course, my own.

79   See above, note 26.

NOTES

80 *Lettres Milanaises*, 86–87.
81 Sections of the article are reprinted in the *Lettres Milanaises*, 80–81.
82 Ibid., 88.
83 Poulin, VII, 63–64.
84 Poulin, VII, 65–67.
85 *Der Turm*, in: *Dramen* IV, 463.
86 *Lettres Milanaises*, 87.
87 Poulin, IX, 58–67.
88 *Lettres Milanaises*, 95.
89 Ibid., 97.
90 Poulin, IX, 55–56.
91 Poulin, IX, 32–34.
92 Cf. Demetz, "Weltinnenraum und Technologie," 9.
93 Fromm, *Escape from Freedom*, 138.
94 Theodor W. Adorno, "Rede über Lyrik und Gesellschaft," in *Noten zur Literatur I* (Frankfurt a.M.: Suhrkamp, 1958), 78–79.
95 Mosse, *The Crisis of German Ideology*, 6.
96 Adorno, "Rede über Lyrik und Gesellschaft," 74.

Chapter 6
Conclusion

1 There is more support for this claim than could possibly be contained in a single annotation. The following seems to me a representative view: Gordon Craig, in "Engagement and Neutrality in Weimar Germany," *Journal of Contemporary History* II (1967): 49, argues that, in opposition to writers in other countries, France in particular, "German men of letters have always had an ambivalent relationship towards society" and he characterizes this as "that well-known *Innerlichkeit* that regarded the external

world and its works as being of no legitimate concern to the artist and that made aesthetic contemplation and intellectual activity ends in themselves."

2 This is the view of the well-known student of the problems of nationalism, Hans Kohn, *Living in a World Revolution* (New York: Trident Press, 1964), pp. 164–165: "Much more than had communism, fascism had rejected everything for which free men stand."

3 Cf. ibid., 130: "The fascist infection began to spread throughout Central Europe and to the Balkans, where a reactionary elite wished to perpetuate an obsolete social order under the pretext of defending society—which meant the status quo. . . . "

4 Salis, *Rainer Maria Rilke: The Years in Switzerland*, 33.

5 George Orwell, *Critical Essays* (London: Secker and Warburg, 1946), 119.

6 Cf. the methodological reflections in the essay by Bernd Peschken, "Literatur und Politik im Wechselverhältnis: Zu Ferdinand Gregorovius' Goethe-Bild 1849. Eine Außenbetrachtung," *Jahrbuch der deutschen Schillergesellschaft* XIV (1970): esp. 488–490.

7 Lucien Goldmann, "Le concept de structure significative en histoire de la culture," in *Recherches dialectiques* (Paris: Gallimard, 1967), 116.

Paris circle. Perhaps, though, influences coming from Valéry's personal acquaintances must be regarded as having been especially effective.

8 The editor of the *Lettres Milanaises* refers to certain possible French influences. A somewhat loose connection might be established to Valery Larbaud, coeditor of Paul Valery's journal *Commerce*, where the first examples of Rilke's French poetry appeared. Valery Larbaud wrote sketches on Italy that were later collected in a book, *Aux Couleurs de Rome* (Paris: Gallimard, 1938) that clearly reveals his inclinations toward fascism. This orientation was

doubtless already evident during Rilke's lifetime. Of course, there were also other profascist acquaintances in Rilke's Paris circle. Perhaps, though, influences coming from Valéry's personal acquaintances must be regarded as having been especially effective.

9 *Briefe an eine junge Frau*, 30.

10 Thomas Mann arrived at similar conclusions. In his essay of 1939 entitled "Culture and Politics" ("Kultur und Politik," in *Altes und Neues. Kleine Prosa aus fünf Jahrzehnten* [Frankfurt a. M.: S. Fischer, 1953] 648) he speaks of the catastrophic consequences of an apolitical attitude and of an arrogant, aristocratic disdain for politics. These are errors that he himself regretted having succumbed to once he had realized "how very much the misery of German history and its path to the cultural catastrophe of National Socialism are connected with the apolitical stance of the bourgeois intellect in Germany."

Index

Adorno, Theodor, 113
Along the Edge of Life, 7
American; Rilke's view of, 66
Andreas-Salomé, Lou, 5, 24, 25
angels: in *Duino Elegies*, 90–91, 111
anglophobia, 60
anomie, 50, 53, 54
anti-semitism, 15, 16, 26, 72–80
 moderate anti-semitism of Rilke, 72, 80
apolitical attitudes, 2, 10, 26, 115
architectural criticism; allusions to, in *Duino Elegies*, 99
art; divorced from the common man, 34
art for art's sake; concept of, 25, 39
atavism, 111–12

Babylon, as symbol of sin, 59
Baudelaire, Pierre Charles, 61
Beatrice Altichieri (character), 17
"Beggar and the Proud Young Lady, The," 17
beggars, 64–66
Benn, Gottfried, 29
Bible, The; concepts from, in *Book of Hours*, 59
Blok, Aleksandr Aleksandrovič, 68–69
Blumenthal-Weiss, Ilse, 76, 79
Bohemia and the Bohemians, 9, 11
Bohusch (character), 13, 22
 strangulation of, 14
Book of Hours, 58, 59

"Caena and Thermal Baths," (lecture by Schuler), 93–94
Catholics, 16

INDEX

Chandos (character by Hofmannsthal), 69–70
Charlotte (character), 7
Chiemsee, 31
Christians and Christianity:
   doctrine of poverty, 17–18, 65
   Rilke's renouncing of, 18
cities and city life, 57–59
Cités et pays suisses (G. Reynold), 109
"City of Pain," 101–2
   carnival setting in, 102
civilization conflicting with culture, 112–13
clerical fascism, 47
communism and the futility of Bolshevism, 103
conservatism and conservatives, 40, 42
craftmanship; disappearance of, 61
Cremonesi, Senator Fillippo, 83
Czechs:
   in Rilke's work, 7–13, 18–22, 82
   soul and character of, 18–19

dead, cult of the, in *Duino Elegies*, 92
death, 92–95
   Schuler's interpretation of, 93–94
democracy:
   emnity for, 104
   ideological shift away from, 41

Diedrichs, Eugen, 86
Dnjepr River, the, 15
Dostoevsky, Feodor; allusions to his characters, 96
Dresden, 74
Duino Elegies, 3, 59, 89–102
   "City of Pain," 101–2
   historical concepts of, 97
Dürer, Albrecht, 86
dwarfs, 64–66

economic concepts borrowed from Reynold, 109
Eisner, Kurt, 36, 38
elitism, 22, 26, 45, 61
Ernst Land (character), 8
European Rightists, 42, 44–45, 47, 80
Ewald (character), 14
Ewald Tragy, 7

fascists and fascism, 3, 22, 23, 28, 42, 45–47, 56, 71–72
   as a foil to instability, 109
   in *Lettres Milanaises*, 102–13
   Italian variety of, 3, 22, 39, 47, 72, 109
Faust II (Goethe), 43
First World War, the, 26, 27, 30–41
   Rilke's activities during, 35–37
Five Songs, 27–30
Florentine Diary, 25
formlessness; concept of, 107
freedom; attack on, in *Lettres Milanaises*, 103

French Revolution, the, 39, 108
Freudianism; condemned by Rilke, 76
Fullerborn, Ulrich, 52

Gallarati-Scotti, Signora, 106–7
Gaulle, Charles de, 86
George, Stefan, 26
Goethe, Johann Wolfgang, 31, 91
Goldmann, Lucien, 117
group action; concept of, 35

Harrison, John R., 105
Heine, Heinrich, 62
Hofmannsthal, Hugo von, 69, 110
Hulewics, Witold von; letters to, 59–60, 106
human existence; concepts of, in *Duino Elegies*, 97

Imperial Union of German Handworkers, the, 63
industrialism, 23, 42–43, 50
  as a form of modernity, 99–102
  attacks on technology in *Lettres Milanaises*, 103
  opinions about, 43–44
intelligentsia, criticism of, 40
internationalism, 42
  Rilke's expression of, 19
  fascist opposition to, 43
invisible transformations in poetry; concept of, 106–7
Italy, 25, 46, 47, 72, 109

Jenny, Rudolph Christoph, 77
Jesuits, 16
Jews: *see* anti-semitism
journeys of Rilke; references to, 25, 27

Kafka, Franz, 91
Khmelniçki, Bogdan, 16
Kiev, 15
"King Bohusch," 9, 14
Kolb, Annette, 67
König, Hertha, 67, 68
Kraus, Karl, 76
Kreuzer, Helmut, 2
"Krummauer Castle," 10

La Russie Epique, 16
Lettres Milanaises, 3, 47, 68, 83, 84, 85, 102–13
  comparison with *Duino Elegies*, 111–13
liberalism:
  attacked in *Sonnets of Orpheus*, 104
  Rilke's views of, 39
Lissauer, Ernst, 75
Luisa (character), 9, 10, 14, 22
  illness of, 11, 18

Machiavelli, Prince Niccolo di Bernardo, 8
Malte, 10, 88
Malte (character), 26, 49, 58
mana, 94
Mann, Thomas, 105–6
marriage, 49
Masaryk, Jan, 82
Mason, Eudo C., 47, 60

INDEX

Matteotti, Giacomo, 3
medievalism, 108
Meerhelm, Colonel Meering von (character), 7, 13, 18
Mehring, Walter, 82
Melchisedech (character), 16, 73
Mewes, Anni: letters to, 39–40
Michelangelo, 26
middle class, the, 45
modernity:
   defined, 52–53
   in conflict with the past, 99–102
   rejection of, 10
monuments of the past; approval of, 99–100
Mühlon, Dr. Wilhelm, 81
Munich, 27, 31, 53
Munich Council, the, 68
   headed by Eisner, 36
   Rilke's early support of, 39
Mussolini, Benito, 3, 46, 47, 71, 83, 84, 111
   regime of, 109
Muzot, 51
mysticism, 21
   death concepts of rightist movements, 93
mythic figures in *Duino Elegies*, 95

Nadherny, Baroness Sidonie, 74
Nazi movement, 16, 45
Notebooks of Malte Laurids Brigge. See Malte

obedience and submission to government, 104
"Of Poverty and of Death," 58–59
"Orphic Theology" (Bachofen), 95
Orwell, George, 116

Paris, 25
Parsons, Talcott, 43
peasants, 15
Philemon (character), 43
plants; treatment of, in *Duino Elegies*, 92
Plato, 106
poets and poetry:
   admiration for Blok, 68
   formlessness, 106–8
   in *Duino Elegies*, 95
   plants as themes of, 48
   rejection of humane themes, 105
   relationship to magic, 106
   symbolism of later works, 95
Poland and the Polish, 15, 16
politics and political concepts:
   contempt for politics of German intellectuals, 114
   political stability, 109–10
   Rilke's superficial view of, 115, 119
   views of the Right, 44–45, 47.
   See also fascists and fascism
Pound, Ezra, 62, 105
poverty, 17, 65–66
press, the, 51

profiteering:
  carnival setting for, in *Duino Elegies*, 102
  in *Lettres Milanaises*, 103
  wartime varieties of, 33
Proust, Marcel, 49
Prussianism, 81
psychic structures; concept of, 6

Rambaud, Alfred, 16
rationalism, 55
Republic, The (Plato), 106
revolution; disenchantment with, 35–39
Reynold, Gonzague de, 109, 117
Rezek (character), 8, 9, 14
Rilke, Rainier Maria:
  approval of facism by, 3, 22, 109
  aversion for city life of, 10, 111
  change of name by, 5
  creative aspect of, 4
  cult of admiration for, 1
  early influences on, 6–7
  Germanophilia, rebellion against, by, 7, 19, 20
  historical ideas of, 97–98
  instability, both mental and social, 48–49
  parents of, 5–6
  period of inactivity of, 30–31
  poems of, 11, 58–59, 60, 89–113
  Prague background of, 5–14
  pretended estrangement from politics of, 2, 10, 26
  progressive aspect of, 13
  reactionary aspect of, 13
  rebellious nature of, 20, 48
  shifting views of, 3, 13, 16, 19–23, 29, 35, 40, 55
  social stability; concepts of, 13, 109–10
Rolland, Romain, 67
romantic concepts; conflict of, with rationalism in *Duino Elegies*, 99
Rosalka (character), 10
Russia, 25
Russian Revolution as symbol of undesirable change, 66, 68

saltimbanquis, the, 92
Sauer, Wolfgang, 43, 45, 46, 56
Savonarola, Girolamo, 8
"Scene from the Venice Ghetto, A," 16
Schnitzler, Arthur, 77
Schuler, Alfred, 93
"Scythians, The" (Blok), 69
Shaw, George Bernard, 67
"Siblings, The," 7, 13, 14, 18, 19
Slavic elements, 7–19
social Darwinism, 65
social deterioration in *Duino Elegies*, 97
social fascism, 47
social reform; ridicule of, in *Book of Hours*, 102
solipsism; persistence of, in Rilke's works, 34, 65

INDEX

solitude; in *Duino Elegies*, 91
"Song of Justice, The," 14, 73
Sonnets to Orpheus, 3, 60, 89, 93, 94, 98
  anti-technology aspects in, 100–101
"Sounds of Freedom," 11–12
Spengler, Oswald, 113
Spinoza, Baruch, 78, 80
status seeking of Rilke and his parents, 6–7
Stifter, Adalbert, 65
Stolp, Count Baudissin zu, 67
Stories of Our Dear Lord, 14, 17, 35, 88
Suttner, Berta von, 85

technology, 59–63, 103
temples; in *Duino Elegies*, 99
Thurn und Taxis, Princess, 73–74, 79
torture; allusion to, in *Sonnets to Orpheus*, 104
Two Stories of Prague, 7, 19, 22, 88, 89

war and war themes, 27–30
  dying for one's country, 85
  general blame for, 32
  Germany's responsibility for WW. I, 81
  journalistic scapegoats, 32
  profiteering from, 33
  Rilke's changing view of, 29–30, 33–35
  wealthy class; partiality for, 67
Weber, Eugen, 46, 95, 107
Weber, Max, 36
"Wegwarten" (Rilke's journal), 63
Werfel, Franz, 73
"Why Our Dear Lord Wants There to Be Poor People," 17
Wilhelm II, 83

Yeats, William Butler, 62, 105

Zdenko Wanka (character), 9, 18
Zionism, 79